101
Managerial Situations
and
How to Handle Them

101
Managerial Situations
and
How to Handle Them

William Wachs

Parker Publishing Company, Inc.
West Nyack, New York

Library of Congress Cataloging in Publication Data

Wachs, William.
    101 managerial situations and how to handle them.

    1. Personnel management. I. Title.
HF5549.W23   658.3   75-38682
ISBN 0-13-635367-3

Printed in the United States of America

Contents

7

How This Book
Can Help You Handle
Vital Managerial Situations

This book offers you experience-tested solutions to many of the problems you face on an ongoing basis. It presents 101 real-life business situations which the author has faced in a wide variety of companies of all kinds and sizes throughout the country. For each case included here there is, in addition to a valid recommendation for handling the situation, a brief discussion of the sound management principles involved and an indication of how similar difficulties can be prevented.

This book was written because of widespread expression by management people of the need for this kind of approach to their constant problems. They knew and understood the basic principles of successful people-management, but they wanted additional help in solving relevant people problems through realistic, applicable examples.

This book is intended primarily for the management employee of any company who is responsible for the profitable results of one or more assistants who, in turn, have assistants of their own. In other words, it is intended primarily for the middle management levels.

It can, however, be valuable to upper management levels if such managers translate the problems (and their solutions) into terms of how they must guide their middle managers in those kinds of situations. It can also help the first-line manager — the foreman, the supervisor, etc. — with comparable problems stemming from his non-management assistants on both wage and salary levels.

The book will benefit you in the following ways:

- It will pinpoint most of the daily people problems you have.
- It will make it easy for you to relate the situations which are presented to your own specific applicable problems.
- It will provide you with a sound suggestion for solutions to those problems, based on broad and valid experience.
- It will give you an opportunity to evaluate your own approach to such situations.
- It will afford you a vehicle for the ready communication to your assistants of your analysis and resolution of situations in which they're involved.
- It will guide you to steps which can prevent the recurrence of the problems presented to you.
- It will refresh your memory of the sound principles of management you already know and may have been too busy to practice.
- It will give you a solid base for helping your assistants or fellows.

This book is different from others on the subject in that:

- It emphasizes the *situation,* rather than the principle, while still developing the principle adequately.
- It is based on problems typical of most businesses, rather than those applicable to only a few kinds of companies.
- It covers practically the entire gamut of people problems which you can face.
- Its suggested solutions to problems are practical, realistic and easy to apply.
- It is easy to read or to refer to, depending on how you need to use it.

The unique features that make this book special are:

1. It groups the problems you face by categories which are easy to identify. For example, if you want to compare

your approach to the problem of the assistant who refuses or fails to evaluate his men accurately, the concept of *authority* is your clue to the Chapter (Two) where the relevant case can be found.

2. It faces up squarely to the realistic needs of a middle manager, pulling no punches. Take, for instance, Chapter Six, which tackles one of the most serious impediments to company profits.

3. It can be used by you as a training aid for your assistants. This is illustrated in Chapter One, where the situations you face are also problems your assistants have, and the same cases can be used by them (under your guidance) as by you.

4. It helps you to decide whether a situation you face is of sufficient importance to warrant your time and attention. This is so because both the group heading (for example: Chapter Four, How to Handle Problems With Fellow Managers) and the specific case title (for example: Where The Personnel Manager Hires a Man for You Without Consulting You) reveal at once whether your applicable situation fits into what the book considers an important problem to be dealt with.

W.W.

1

How to Handle
Resistance to Change

In the following situations notice how the manager first ascertains what is being resisted and why. Observe how this leads him to a feasible solution which, at the same time, provides the best approach to motivating acceptance.

SITUATION NUMBER 1 — Resistance to change by the supervisor who insists on doing it the old way.

INCIDENT

Frank Rankin was the company's maintenance manager. The operations manager, Pete Senner, often noticed that either Frank or one of his foremen was nowhere to be found at a particular time during the working hours. Pete asked Frank why this was so. Frank told Pete that on those occasions one or another of those missing was in town buying a needed part.

When Pete asked Frank why he didn't follow the newly established requisition procedure, Frank replied that he'd always sent someone — or gone himself — because it was quicker than any requisition procedure.

ALTERNATE SOLUTIONS

A. Pete can thank Frank for the information and tell him that he'll discuss the situation with him later. Pete then ask his controller to gather together for him the necessary figures to show Frank how it costs the company more money to do it *his* way than through the established procedure. Pete can then appeal to Frank to subordinate his well-intentioned impatience to the realities of maximum/optimum profitability.

THE ESSENCE OF THIS APPROACH

Pete relies on facts and figures to overcome a resistance to change based on a preference for the comfort of the old ways regardless of the effect on the company.

B. Pete can begin at once to ask Frank questions like these:

- How long does it take for a foreman to get a part in town personally as compared with the time it takes to fill out a requisition and send it in?
- With the proper planning, why isn't the requisition procedure just as effective?
- What does it cost the company in nonproductive time when a foreman is away from his post?
- How much can the company lose in productivity when a foreman isn't supervising his workers?

Pete can then ask Frank whether he doesn't agree that the new way is better for both Frank and the company, and ask him to give it a try.

THE ESSENCE OF THIS APPROACH

Pete leads Frank to thinking the situation through in an orderly fashion and arriving at a desirable conclusion of his own which he would more willingly put into practice.

ADAPTING THE SOLUTIONS TO YOUR OWN WORK

Whenever you come across supervisors who are obviously doing things the old way despite a new way which has been firmly established and effectively communicated, you might want to tackle the problem somewhat along these lines:

- Find out why he's using the old way, either by asking him or by observation.
- Make sure that he knows and fully understands the new way and the valid reasons behind it.
- Get him to realize that the old way is less profitable for the company and, if possible, show him that it's not as beneficial to him.
- Try appealing to his strong sense of loyalty to the company and his interest in the company's success.
- In any event, make sure he promises to follow the new approach.
- Above all, follow up to see whether he does.

SITUATION NUMBER 2 — Resistance to change by the employee who has always come to work late.

INCIDENT

Alf Cabot lived about 20 miles from the company's location and drove to work, in his own car and alone, every day when the office was open. All office employees were due to start work at 8 A.M. Alf generally arrived at about 8:05 and didn't actually start his work until around 8:15.

Alf had been working for the company for some 20 years. Alf's immediate superior, a relatively new supervisor, was Bob Dabney. Bob finally got around to dealing with Alf's persistent tardiness. One day he asked Alf whether he couldn't make an effort to be ready to work every business day at 8 A.M.

Alf replied that if he left his home any earlier than he normally did, the traffic would be lighter and he would get to the office around 7:45, which was too early. The reason that he was always late was that by leaving his house considerably later than that he hit a great deal of traffic, which was what delayed him. He concluded that he didn't want to have to rise too early or waste time at the office before 8 A.M.

ALTERNATE SOLUTIONS

A. Bob can rearrange Alf's official working hours to run from 8:15 A.M. to 4:15 P.M. and insist that Alf be consistently punctual on that schedule. Under this solution it would also be important for Bob to make sure that all the other employees who come into contact with Alf, or know about him, understand the new schedule and accept the reasons for it as being valid *only* for Alf.

THE ESSENCE OF THIS APPROACH

If Bob can be sure that none of the other employees will think Alf is receiving special treatment (and Alf can really be satisfactorily productive under that schedule) Bob has preserved the important principle of punctuality and has kept an older employee happy.

B. Bob can make a survey of all the people under his responsibility to find out what beginning time is best for all or most of them, paying special attention to the matter of traffic at different times in the morning. If he finds that all or most of them would prefer the earlier time and that this wouldn't materially interfere with the efficient running of the rest of the office and/or company, he could request the corresponding change in time from the proper management employee in the company.

THE ESSENCE OF THIS APPROACH

All of the employees involved get a feeling of participation, under controlled conditions, in an important decision, and are permitted a measure of personal convenience without interfering with company efficiency. Of course, if a sufficient number found the earlier time inconvenient, this solution would not be wise.

C. Bob can insist that the overall needs of the company have been validly established as calling for the present hours, emphasize that there can be no exceptions and try to sell Alf on changing his attitude and habits. Among the things he can say are:

- Everyone knows how loyal and conscientious Alf has been for so many years.
- Alf's contribution to the company's continued success is well recognized and appreciated by all.
- Bob cannot make any exceptions in the schedule because this would inevitably lead to friction and poor morale.
- Bob knows that Alf will want to make yet another sacrifice for the company to which he is so devoted.
- Alf can use the new company lounge to relax if he gets to work too early to start work.

THE ESSENCE OF THIS APPROACH

Bob preserves the uniformity of adherence to an unchangeable company policy; appeals to Alf's sense of pride, contribution and loyalty, and tries to make Alf feel that it isn't really too hard to adjust to the required schedule.

ADAPTING THE SOLUTIONS TO YOUR OWN WORK

Whenever you encounter an employee who has *always* (or generally) come to work late (even if it's only by a few minutes each time), touch base with as many of the following considerations as are applicable:

- First try to get at the *real* reason for his tardiness, and if that reason is relatively unimportant to him, see if you can easily make him agree that that reason is less important to him than regular punctuality.
- If you can't convince him that his reason is insignificant, see whether you can make a change for him which will not interfere with company efficiency or morale and if you can, make the required allowance for him.

- If, however, it's best for the company for him to conform, try to sell him on this by appealing to his better motives and trying to make him comfortable with the change.

Of course, if he won't buy your efforts and he simply must conform, you'll have to be firm and apply normal steps for dealing with an employee who simply will not follow company policy.

SITUATION NUMBER 3 — Resistance to change by the assistant who keeps asking you to solve his problems.

INCIDENT

Roger Abbey was in charge of the assembly section of a plant. His work depended in large measure on the smooth and steady flow of components from the section just before his in the established plan of operation for manufacturing.

At least two or three times a week Roger would come in to see his immediate superior, Cy Rollins, to complain that either he didn't get his materials on time, that they were of generally unacceptable quality or that he had to ask for certain components which should have arrived without any special request.

In each case, Cy's investigations revealed that Roger never spoke first to the foreman in charge of the other section to ask for what was needed or to request a general improvement in the flow.

ALTERNATE SOLUTIONS

A. Cy can ask Roger and the other foreman, Jim Eagle, to meet with him. He can then explain to Jim that Roger claims to have a problem which Cy would like the two of them to try to work out together to the satisfaction of all concerned. Cy then asks Roger to explain the difficulty, listens to Jim's side of the story, tries to straighten out the problem and asks the two of them to try to make all necessary adjustments in the future, consulting him only if it's really necessary.

THE ESSENCE OF THIS APPROACH

Cy tries to find out what the real problem is, makes an effort to get the two of them to resolve their differences between them, but still leaves the door open for seeking *his* help.

B. Cy tells Roger that he'll look into the situation and let him know his solution later. Cy then talks to Jim and gets his side of the story. If there's a serious difference of opinion on what the true situation is, Cy can bring the two of them together as in solution A. If, however, Cy is able to arrive at all necessary facts, he urges Jim to do his best along proper lines and assures Roger that this will be done. He then asks Roger to go directly to Jim whenever a problem of the same sort arises, to try to settle the matter between them, coming to him (Cy) only when this isn't possible.

THE ESSENCE OF THIS APPROACH

By going to Jim first — privately — Cy can get Jim's version of the story without the strain which might result from what could be an antagonistic situation.

C. Cy can ask Roger whether he has first gone to Jim to discuss the matter. If Roger says that he hasn't, Cy can insist that Roger do so, telling him that the reason for his insistence is that an important facet of an assistant's job is a willingness and ability to solve most of his problems by himself.

THE ESSENCE OF THIS APPROACH

An assistant must be told that he must work and speak with all other employees involved in the work flow; he must be able to get along with them and resolve mutual problems. The assistant must appeal to his immediate superior for help only when his persuasiveness, authority or resources make it unprofitable for the company for him to refrain from going up one rung in the ladder.

ADAPTING THE SOLUTIONS TO YOUR OWN WORK

In the orientation and refresher training that you provide to your assistants you must always make plain to them that:

- The very nature of their jobs as part of management requires that they try to solve as many of their own problems as possible, without coming to you.
- They may, of course, feel free to come to you with their problems if they feel that either they should not or cannot solve them by themselves, or that they aren't sure that they can.
- When they do come to you, they should do so armed with all the facts and ready to offer alternate or preferred solutions.

Then whenever one of your assistants does come to you for help in solving one of his problems, you should:

- Give him all the help he needs if he was justified in coming to you, telling him that this was an example of justification, and why.
- Not offer to help him if you believe that he should solve the problem himself, asking him to go back and try again on his own.

You can't spare the time from your own work to solve your subordinates' problems. Besides, if you do, you may never develop that aspect of their managerial skills to your satisfaction.

It's far better for an assistant to make the wrong decision in a given situation — and be properly corrected by you so he can do better the next time — than never to learn how to make wise decisions.

SITUATION NUMBER 4 — Resistance to change by the two men who never got along with each other.

INCIDENT

Andy Marple headed the company's equipment reconditioning department. John Sterne managed the Services of Supply section. Both reported to Paul Myers.

For a long time, a typical occurrence practically every day was something like this: a reconditioning worker would get a requisition for a needed tool or part signed by Andy and take it to the supply room. He'd hand it to the clerk on duty and have to wait almost half an hour before getting what he needed.

Andy's people kept reporting to him that the reason for this was that the clerks continually said that the requisition was not sufficiently detailed to enable them to find what was being requested easily.

Andy finally went to see John and angrily demanded that this practice be stopped at once. John retorted, with equal ire, that all that it would take would be a more accurate description of the parts or tools requested, in keeping with the system that John followed for his storage. Andy's reply was that John should make a greater effort to understand the speed with which Andy's men needed those items and supply them more rapidly, since the delays were slowing up the work of reconditioning and costing the company a great deal of money.

When John refused to budge from his position, Andy came to Paul and told him that he just couldn't work with John and that Paul had better move one of them to a different job.

ALTERNATE SOLUTIONS

A. Paul can examine the forms used for the requisition and see what provision is made for describing the tools and parts requested. He can then ask John to point out in what specific respects that caption fails to meet the needs of John's clerks, if they are to fill the requisitions most speedily. He can then ask Andy what objections, if any, he has to John's suggestions. Paul can then resolve, on his own, any differences that still exist and have the form redesigned accordingly.

THE ESSENCE OF THIS APPROACH

Paul goes immediately and directly to the heart of the stated complaint, gets the opinions of both parties involved regarding the solution to the problem and makes his own decision utilizing as much as he can of their suggestions. He follows up with immediate action.

B. Paul calls Andy and John together and holds a meeting with them along these lines:

Paul first makes statements like these:

- I've called you together because there seems to be a difference of opinion between you on an important matter of procedure.
- I value each of you equally. Each of you is very competent and conscientious in his own job.
- The very nature of your respective responsibilities is such that you must both work together smoothly in the interests of the profitability of our department.
- Now I'd like each one of you, in turn, to tell me what he thinks the problem is.

Paul then asks Andy to start, requesting that John not interrupt. Paul makes careful notes while Andy talks. Paul then does the same regarding John, and asks either of them any questions he feels advisable in order to get as much data as possible.

Paul then thanks both of them, asks them to try to resolve the problem as best they can until he can get back to them and adjourns the meeting with thanks.

Paul personally investigates the flow of work, following several requisitions through from beginning to end. Paul then decides on any changes in the requisition (and/or the procedure) which he deems called for and asks Andy and John to meet with him again. This time he makes sure to get the following points across:

- There was justification for both sides and he appreciates their having brought the matter to his attention.
- He has come up with a solution for the problem, and explains it to them.
- If they still have suggestions, he listens to them, tries to incorporate as many as he can and then tells them exactly how he wants the matter handled.
- He appeals to them to try the new method out and let him know if there are any more snags.
- He assures them that he knows that there is no personal animosity between them and that they will make the new

method work in their usual objective and cooperative manner.

Paul follows up from time to time to see whether the problem has been solved and takes whatever additional steps may be necessary.

THE ESSENCE OF THIS APPROACH

1. Paul starts the solution with a joint discussion, leading to a sense of consultation and participation.
2. He emphasizes from the start his high opinion of each of them.
3. He makes no mention of any subjective emotional possibility underlying the problem.
4. He appeals to their positive attitudes regarding the company.
5. He gets each man's uninterrupted version of the situation.
6. He investigates and comes up with a proposed solution, giving them another chance to comment, and tells them how he wants them to cooperate.
7. He follows up.

ADAPTING THE SOLUTIONS TO YOUR OWN WORK

When two or more of your men complain to you about their inability to get along with each other, no matter how they put it, the first thing you should do is try to get at the real reasons for that feeling. This is sometimes best accomplished by individual meetings with each of them, sometimes by joint meetings and sometimes by a combination of the two methods.

In all cases you'd do well to make them feel that the problem is strictly operational, completely ignoring anything personal that they may say or imply. Get their opinions; tell them you'll investigate; do so and arrive at your own conclusions.

If it turns out that the problem is an inalterable personality clash, you may have to put one or both of them in different jobs, where they don't have to work together. If, however, the problem

is really operational (which has led to the personality clash, if any),
try to make them feel that your solution represents a compromise
between their excellent suggestions, be firm about what you want
them to do and express complete confidence that they will jointly
make the thing work and follow up from time to time to see that
it does.

SITUATION NUMBER 5 — Resistance to change by the worker who is indifferent to safety rules.

INCIDENT

Mary Jenkins works in the office. She is a highly competent, hard-working, loyal employee. She is, however, accustomed
to taking short cuts and likes to avoid doing anything which interferes with the speedy and efficient flow of her work.

Her desk is so situated that there is just about enough room
to get past it to go from one part of the office to another. She has
a number of important files in the two long drawers at the bot-
tom of each side of the desk and has to consult them frequently
while at work. She almost always leaves one or another — or
both — of these drawers fully open while she's using those files.

The company's manual on policies and procedures, in its
section on safety in the office, clearly states that this practice is
hazardous and therefore forbidden.

On a number of occasions, Alice Babcock, Mary's supervisor, has noticed this repeated unsafe practice by Mary and decides that the time has come to do something about it. Alice,
therefore, calls it to Mary's attention. Mary agrees that Alice is
right and closes the open drawer at that time; but Mary soon for-
gets and repeats the violation several times, even though Alice
reminds her about it several times also.

ALTERNATE SOLUTIONS

A. Alice can make it her business to walk by Mary's desk
when one of the drawers is open, carefully pretend to bump her
leg against the open drawer, show pain and call this to Mary's
attention, emphasizing that that could happen — and more

seriously — to someone else as long as Mary continues this habit.

THE ESSENCE OF THIS APPROACH

It could bring forcefully to Mary's attention the seriousness of her negligence and, perhaps, sufficiently impress her to change her habits.

B.   Alice can ask Mary to come into Alice's office for a chat. At that conference Alice could make statements along these lines:

- Mary, we both know that you're conscientious and competent.
- I've spoken to you several times about the hazardous practice you engage in by leaving the desk drawers wide open.
- I cannot permit this practice to continue for two reasons: it's liable to cause accidents, and it's against company policy and procedure.
- What are we going to do about this?

THE ESSENCE OF THIS APPROACH

1. Alice has specifically made Mary aware of Alice's displeasure with this act, against a background of appreciation of Mary's general performance.
2. Alice has made it clear that Mary has done *two* wrong things: created a safety hazard and violated the company policy.
3. Alice appeals to Mary's ability and/or willingness to make the effort necessary to break the undesirable habit.

C.   If solution B. doesn't work, Alice will have to tell Mary that her repeated failure to abide by the company's policies and procedures must be subjected to normal discipline practices, despite Mary's important contributions to the company. If this doesn't yield the desired results, Alice must keep her promise.

THE ESSENCE OF THIS APPROACH

Alice tries to convince Mary that she simply must abide by the rules and that, if she doesn't, her general excellence does not permit her to violate company rules.

ADAPTING THE SOLUTIONS TO YOUR OWN WORK

Any company rule must either be followed by all employees or (if it is deemed an unwise rule) abrogated. As long as a company rule is official it must be enforced with respect to *all* employees, regardless of how well any of them perform their duties otherwise. This is because the rule in itself must be followed for the reasons for which it was established, because failure to enforce it with one employee may lead to its abuse by another and because a supervisor's failure to enforce rules undermines his authority.

The preceding solutions to safety problems are therefore applicable to any situations where an employee consistently fails to abide by rules. In calling the violation to the attention of an employee, you should wherever possible begin by praising the positive aspects of his work; then carefully point out the rule and its violation, stress the absolute nature of the requirement to conform, and appeal to the employee to take the necessary steps to correct the situation. If this fails, you must insist on compliance, having recourse to discipline if all else fails. If you don't, not only will that employee become an uncontrollable maverick but he will probably serve as a model for others.

SITUATION NUMBER 6 — Resistance to change by the foreman who insists on fraternizing with his men.

INCIDENT

Kurt Faber was a wage employee of great skill, conscientiousness and loyalty. When one of the foremen was retiring from the company, Kurt was made foreman by the department superintendent, Earl Berson.

Kurt had been very friendly and popular with his fellow wage-earners. When he became a foreman over them he didn't in any way change his demeanor, attitudes or method of speaking with them. He still socialized with them both in the plant and on the outside.

Earl noticed that Kurt was constantly covering up for any of his men who failed to do what they were supposed to. Kurt never reported any of them for infractions of discipline and let them get away with some infractions.

While Kurt generally did a good job, his department's productivity was slightly below standard and some of the other foremen were complaining that they couldn't enforce the rules and standards on their own men that Kurt neglected with his men.

ALTERNATE SOLUTIONS

A. Earl can take Kurt aside at a convenient and relaxed time and:

- Point out to him the laxness and low productivity in his department.
- Relate it to Kurt's inability or unwillingness to be firm with his men.
- Explain that this is due to his fraternizing habits.
- Ask him to gradually wean himself away from being their *friend* and become their *leader*.

THE ESSENCE OF THIS APPROACH

Earl comes right to the point and asks Kurt to make the required change on a gradual basis.

B. Earl takes Kurt aside — again leisurely and privately — and tells him:

- In every company there are two kinds of employees: management and non-management. This is so because of the very nature of the business world.
- It's management's job to get maximum/optimum productivity from non-management, consistent with decency and ethics.
- Many non-management people unconsciously — if not consciously — fail to exert themselves consistently to

their fullest and best capacities. It's management's job to motivate them toward that kind of effort.

- While there are many facets to effective motivation, the non-management employee must be made to realize that he has to yield certain results even if he can't be motivated into them.
- A foreman's fraternization with his men makes it difficult for him to insist and be forceful where this is necessary, as it so frequently is.
- If Kurt wants to continue as a foreman, he must consistently get the kind of results which can come only from the proper combination of fairness, consideration and decency with firmness.
- Kurt simply must wean himself away from fraternization and replace it by the proper kind of respect for and interest in his employees.

THE ESSENCE OF THIS APPROACH

- Earl goes into a fairly deep discussion of the management principles involved.
- This not only makes the point but also:
  — Adds to Kurt's general management education.
  — Tends to convince Kurt more readily of the point involved.
- Earl then indicates firmly that Kurt *must* comply.

C. Earl can explain to Kurt the problems that have arisen and probably will continue to arise from Kurt's unwillingness — perhaps inability — to draw the necessary line between himself and his fellows/friends. While praising Kurt's general ability and performance as a foreman, he points out that Kurt will be more effective among men with whom he hadn't worked prior to becoming a foreman.

He then tells Kurt that he will be transferred as a foreman, to another department, where he won't have the same problem — unless Kurt turns out to be unable to resist the habit to fraternize with *any* non-management people. In this case he'll be removed from the rank of foreman (and probably dismissed from the company because it is not good management to demote a man).

THE ESSENCE OF THIS APPROACH

Kurt is removed from the basic temptation which is so natural to men: to want to continue a previous relationship. He is then given an opportunity to be useful to the company (and himself) in a circumstance where that temptation may not exist.

ADAPTING THE SOLUTIONS TO YOUR OWN WORK

Valid management experience has shown that it is a very common tendency for men who have been made foremen over their previous peers to be unable to avoid the same kind of fraternization that they enjoyed as a peer. This should serve as a caution to avoid promoting good workers to foremen over the same men whose peers they were.

2

How to Handle
The Failure to
Use Authority Properly

In the following situations notice how the manager makes sure, first, to ascertain the reason for the failure. He then sees to it that his assistants understand and accept that he (the manager) wants them to have all the authority that they need in order to meet effectively their responsibilities and accountability. Finally, note how he shows them where their actions/inaction result from their failure to exercise properly that authority.

SITUATION NUMBER 7 — The failure to use authority properly by the assistant who bypasses you.

INCIDENT

Larry Andrews is a clerk in the company office. His immediate superior is Tom Linsay. Tom reports directly to Ted Greene. Larry has been an employee of the company for over twenty years, as has Ted. Tom has been with it for only five years. When the company was smaller, Larry used to work directly under Ted, and continued to do so until Ted was promoted and Tom was brought in to take his place.

Larry frequently goes to see Ted in the latter's office, without seeking Tom's approval and without notifying Ted. During those meetings Larry often asks Ted's permission to do certain things, and Ted generally goes along with this without telling Tom.

Larry often presents work to Tom which the latter didn't authorize or which is not done the way Tom wanted it, in both cases situations where Ted had approved the activity or technique. Also, occasionally, when Tom asks Larry to do something for him, Larry says the task will have to wait until he finishes the assignment Ted had given him.

ALTERNATE SOLUTIONS

A. Tom can ask Ted not to receive Larry, accept his suggestions or assign work to him, explaining why.

THE ESSENCE OF THIS APPROACH

It's difficult to get Larry to recognize and accept Tom's authority in complete substitution for Ted's, while Ted, who is more mature and in a higher position, is more apt to recognize the error of his ways and avoid repetitions of this bypassing.

B. Tom can sit down with Larry and go through this chain of ideas:

- We all know how capable, conscientious and loyal you are.
- I also recognize that you used to work with Ted directly.
- Our company must be run on an organized basis.
- This requires strict adherence to chain of command.
- You must communicate only with me as distinguished from Ted.

THE ESSENCE OF THIS APPROACH

Tom explains to Larry the concept involved, in the expectation that this will further motivate him to follow it. Tom also makes it plain that Larry *must* follow the rule.

C. Tom can ask Ted whether he'd like to have Larry assigned to him once more, Tom seeking and getting Larry's replacement for Tom.

THE ESSENCE OF THIS APPROACH

Tom would bring the problem to Ted's attention in a forceful manner, so that Ted would know that Tom means business and won't tolerate a continuation of the improper relationship and practice.

ADAPTING THE SOLUTIONS TO YOUR OWN WORK

Don't under any circumstances permit any one of your assistants to bypass you by going over your head to your immediate superior. Make it plain to all of your assistants that they have the right to appeal any of your decisions they find unacceptable, and what the procedure for so doing is. Tell them, also, that you're always open to suggestions from them. If, however, any of them insist on bypassing you, decide whether it's best in the given situation to solve the problem by dealing with the bypasser alone, the one who was improperly consulted alone, or both of them.

SITUATION NUMBER 8 — The failure to use authority properly by the office manager who blames you for his orders to employees.

INCIDENT

Don Kadin is an office manager, reporting directly to Ken Nack. Don is a knowledgeable, capable and hard-working employee but he has a number of ideas on office management which are at distinct variance with Ken's.

Ken has heard reliable reports that Don, on occasion, will handle a particular situation like this:

- Don will ask one of his people to follow a certain procedure in a stated way.

- His clerk will question the wisdom of that way.
- Don will say: "I agree with you, but don't blame *me. Ken* wants it done that way."

ALTERNATE SOLUTIONS

A. Ken can tell Don what he has heard and ask Don to stop acting that way because it adds to the employee's discontent with company procedure. Ken can add that if Don continues to speak that way Don will have to be transferred to a job where he doesn't manage people.

THE ESSENCE OF THIS APPROACH

Ken lays it right on the line with Don and warns him not to repeat his improper action or he will be put into a less desirable position.

B. Ken can speak to Don in this manner:

- I have it on reliable information that, when you don't like my insistence on certain things being done by your people in a certain way, you tell them — if they complain about it — that you agree with them and blame me for it.
- As you know, whenever you disagree with my instructions to you I welcome your suggestions and try to accept as many of them as I can.
- Do you know the effect that your blaming me has on your people?

Ken then makes sure that Don understands that that kind of shift of responsibility causes the employee to feel that Don doesn't really have any authority over his people and tends to weaken his ability to manage them properly. Ken then insists, while warning that Don's persistence in this undesirable practice will force Ken to transfer Don, that the latter must always act as follows:

- When he disagrees with one of Ken's instructions, he must immediately say so to Ken and offer a counter proposal.
- Whatever Ken finally decides he wants Don to do, Don

must enforce enthusiastically, no matter how he feels about it.

- If one of Don's employees complains about the order, Don must try to sell the employee on its wisdom and, if he can't, must say something like this: "I'm sorry you don't agree with me, but I've told you to do it that way because it's the best way and, therefore, company policy. That's the way you'll have to do it. What's more, you'll have to do it well."

THE ESSENCE OF THIS APPROACH

Ken tries to educate Don to a very important management concept of the proper use of authority, which Don has been violating, at the same time that he tells Don what will happen if he doesn't follow it.

ADAPTING THE SOLUTIONS TO YOUR OWN WORK

Keep on the lookout for the assistant who doesn't like your way of doing things and so informs his people when they complain about having to do them that way. Make sure that you have specific incidents to communicate to your erring assistant, point out to him that he is only hurting his own success with his people and that he *must* issue *your* instructions as though they were his own. He cannot otherwise be effective in his present job and must be relieved of authority.

SITUATION NUMBER 9 — The failure to use authority properly by the purchasing agent who disregards your policies.

INCIDENT

Fred Obler is the general manager of one of the company's plants. Strictly local purchasing needs are handled by the plant's purchasing agent, Barry Hagerty.

Fred has established a written policy and procedure regarding the use of purchase orders and the method of getting them filled. This has been communicated to all concerned, both in the purchasing section and in the plant.

From time to time, when Fred is walking through the plant, he notices that one worker or another — and occasionally a foreman — is missing from his work station. When he asks the superintendent where the missing employee is, the answer is that he's in town picking up a needed part.

When Fred asks Barry about this, his reply is generally that the foreman needed the part at once and Barry okayed his going after it himself, instead of following the normal procedure of having the purchasing section see to it that the part is obtained and delivered to the shop without causing a shop employee to leave his productive work.

ALTERNATE SOLUTIONS

A. Fred can ask the superintendent to refrain from asking the purchasing agent to violate the official procedure, and see to it that his foreman and their men do likewise. He can insist that they do their planning and requisitioning sufficiently in advance to be able to get what they need in the established manner. He can allow exceptions only with his approval.

THE ESSENCE OF THIS APPROACH

Fred removes the temptation from Barry to relinquish his authority for a colleague.

B. Fred can tell Barry that under no circumstances is he to authorize anyone outside of his own section to go after needed items without his — Fred's — permission.

THE ESSENCE OF THIS APPROACH

Fred puts a stop to the practice which is causing the purchasing agent's failure to exercise his authority properly.

C. Fred can call a meeting of the superintendent, the purchasing agent and himself. He can then bring up and discuss the following points:

- The policy and procedure regarding going after needed items has been established in order to promote profitable efficiency, since each employee would then be yielding maximum/optimum productivity from his special skills.
- Sudden trips into town cost unnecessary money.
- In case of a real emergency Fred can always make provisions for getting a needed item fast.
- Only by each employee's consistent exercise of only his own authority can company business be profitably conducted.

Fred would then ask the superintendent to convey this message to his foremen, for them and their men.

THE ESSENCE OF THIS APPROACH

Both sections are exposed simultaneously to the same message, with complete managerial rationale.

ADAPTING THESE SOLUTIONS TO YOUR OWN WORK

The only way to run a profitable purchasing function is to have a purchasing department which is the sole agency for getting what is needed by others in the company. Establish an effective procedure for requisitions, supplier evaluation, purchase orders, delivery and distribution and insist on its being followed. It almost never pays to take a production worker or foreman away from his highly paid work so that he can serve as a messenger.

SITUATION NUMBER 10 — The failure to use authority properly by the department head who marks everybody satisfactory.

INCIDENT

Henry Taft has seven employees under him. He, in turn, reports directly to Ron Illman.

Their company has a semiannual performance review, using a form which, in addition to providing captions for specific evaluations, leads up to an overall rating by each department head for each of his assistants of either satisfactory, outstanding or unsatisfactory.

Ron has repeatedly stressed to all of his department heads, including Ron, that the ratings must be thoroughly accurate and objective. Henry, however, almost always contrives to turn in reports which mark his men uniformly *satisfactory,* with the apparent necessary substantiation.

ALTERNATE SOLUTIONS

A. Ron can sit down with Henry and point out to him the following:

- To have a total number of employees in any one department who are never either outstanding or unsatisfactory defies all validly established laws of probability.
- The only conclusion that Ron can draw is therefore that either Henry is a poor judge of his assistants' performance or he is unwilling — probably because he wants to be popular or because he is afraid to "stick his neck out" — to properly exercise his authority to judge and rate them.
- Ron must decide what Henry's *real* reason is for this failure so that it can be eliminated or so that Ron can conclude that Henry is lacking in that ability to exercise his authority properly.

THE ESSENCE OF THIS APPROACH

Ron emphasizes the probability that Henry's practice is unjustifiable and tries to find out its cause, with a view toward either motivating a capable Henry to improve or deciding that Henry isn't fit for the job.

B. Ron can call his department heads together and make the following explanation/demonstration:

- Tell them that some of them rate *all* of their assistants satisfactory, at least from time to time.
- Point out how important it is to apply the ratings accurately.

- Indicate that he finds it difficult to believe that any group of assistants can be uniformly *only* satisfactory.
- Say that he wants to perform an experiment in that connection.
- List on a visual ten different characteristics of a department head.
- Ask all of them to stand in the rear of the room.
- Take one of the characteristics at a time. For each one, ask them to sit down in a different, designated part of the room according to their own assessment of how they rate with regard to it: satisfactory, outstanding or unsatisfactory.
- After the tenth, ask how many stayed in the satisfactory section for all ten.
- Conclude that the same differences among them for their characteristics must apply to the differences among their assistants for the latter's characteristics.

THE ESSENCE OF THIS APPROACH

Ron forcefully illustrates the improbability of rating uniformity without embarrassing Henry.

C. Ron can take the latest of Henry's evaluations and go over each of them with Henry. Knowing Henry's men quite well, Ron can point out in each case where he disagrees with Henry's evaluation and emphasize that his — Ron's — judgment is accurate and therefore, that any significant difference on Henry's part must of necessity represent his failure to exercise his authority properly, whether for lack of willingness or for lack of ability, either condition calling for correction or decision of inadequacy for the job.

THE ESSENCE OF THIS APPROACH

Ron demonstrates his own ability effectively to evaluate Henry's ability to exercise his authority properly, thus strengthening Ron's authoritativeness in the matter.

ADAPTING THESE SOLUTIONS TO YOUR OWN WORK

If you have a formal performance evaluation program it must be properly administered if it is to be used at all. There is a normal tendency on the part of many assistants to be unwilling to mark anyone unsatisfactory because either it may make them unpopular with their men (which is an untenable attitude on the assistant's part) or it might reflect adversely on their managerial ability (which may be their immediate superior's fault).

Many assistants, also, hesitate to mark any of their men outstanding either for fear of being "shown up" by a "superior" employee or because they fear that such a rating — not immediately followed up by some kind of increase or promotion — could lead to low morale.

You must make sure that you don't substantiate any of these fears; then make it perfectly clear to all of your assistants that:

- It's almost impossible for any one of them to be accurate and objective if he consistently marks *all* of his men satisfactory only.
- A continuation of that practice by any of them has to mean that either they are unwilling properly to exercise that kind of authority or they are incapable of doing so, where either situation must lead to action by you to retain in those positions only those assistants who can consistently exercise it properly.

SITUATION NUMBER 11 — The failure to use authority properly by the engineer who refuses to delegate.

INCIDENT

Carl Wade is an estimating engineer, with ten draftsmen under him. He reports to Gene Sabel. Gene frequently notices that Carl is doing drafting work while several of his men are relatively idle. When Gene has asked Carl whether he is aware of the situation Carl replies:

"Oh, no. My men are always very busy. The drafting work I

do is of the kind that they cannot do properly and must be done only by me."

Gene has investigated and has concluded that with the proper explanation by Carl, his men could do *that* work just as effectively as Carl can.

ALTERNATE SOLUTIONS

A. Gene talks to Carl along these lines:

- Your job is to *manage* your men. Whatever drafting there is has to be done by them. If any of your men are incapable of doing the work properly, recommend their removal from your department.
- While you are doing drafting work yourself you are neglecting two of your own most vital exercises of authority:
    - You can't possibly be doing well work which only you must do.
    - Your relatively unsupervised men are not yielding the most profitable productivity, at unnecessary cost to us.
- You simply must exercise your delegating authority more effectively or you are failing in your responsibility as a manager.

THE ESSENCE OF THIS APPROACH

Gene re-emphasized the nature of Carl's management job, gives him every opportunity to do it well and insists that it must be done well if Carl is to continue to be considered as satisfactory — if not outstanding — in his work.

B. Gene asks Carl to draw up for him a detailed description of Carl's judgment of his duties. Gene then studies this and sits down with Carl to go over it.

Gene explains, and tries to convince Carl, that certain items on Carl's list don't belong to a manager, and that Carl has left out others that do belong to him. Gene lists or checks off any items on which they cannot agree and:

- Insists that Gene's assessment of Carl's management job is accurate.
- Urges Carl to adjust accordingly.
- Stresses that he — Gene — will follow up on Carl's improvement and will take it very seriously if Carl doesn't improve.

THE ESSENCE OF THIS APPROACH

Gene goes back to basics about Carl's management job, tries to sell Carl on them and, where he can't seem to convince him, makes it plain that Carl simply must accept and apply Gene's viewpoint.

ADAPTING THESE SOLUTIONS TO YOUR OWN WORK

Make sure that you frequently supervise at all levels of your authority, without of course undermining your assistant's authority. Whenever you discover less than acceptable productivity among lower levels, find out why this is going on. Where the reason is that one of your own assistants (or *his* assistants) is not using his own authority properly because he refuses to delegate:

- Find out why he refuses to do so.
- Tell him what you've found out.
- Try to motivate him to change his habits.
- To the extent that you can't so motivate him, tell him he simply must comply or else be admitting that he doesn't deserve to continue as a manager.

SITUATION NUMBER 12 — The failure to use authority properly by your boss who gives you responsibility without authority.

INCIDENT

Bernie Jablon is accountable to Bill Kadin. Bill has asked Bernie to be responsible for the productivity of Bernie's hourly employees according to established minimum acceptable standards effectively communicated to Bernie by Bill.

One of Bernie's assistants has consistently failed to meet those standards despite Bernie's very effective efforts at:

- Assigning to him only that work which represents the least he can do in order to justify his filling that job.
- Explaining to him carefully what he's expected to do.
- Training him properly to do the job satisfactorily.
- Providing him with all the necessary facilities in the right way.
- Motivating him properly.

Bernie has all the documentation necessary to prove that that assistant cannot consistently meet those minimum acceptable standards because he is too old for the kind of job involved and additionally, is too set in his ways to be psychologically capable of conforming to the newer production techniques and requirements.

Bernie has asked Bill to have that man taken out of his department (no matter how he is otherwise taken care of by the company) and replaced by someone who will help Bernie meet his accountability to Bill.

Bill has refused, saying that the employee deserves special consideration because of his years of loyal service and real desire to conform, asking Bernie to do the best he can.

When Bernie presents his monthly production reports to Bill they are always deficient in the work done by that man and by others whose work depends on his productivity.

When Bill complains to Bernie about the less-than-desirable results, and Bernie repeats his position regarding that one man, Bill refuses to accept this explanation and insists that the results must be better the next time.

ALTERNATE SOLUTIONS

A. Bernie can tell Bill that he is being unfair and that Bill is, in effect, giving him responsibility/accountability without the necessary, concomitant authority. He can insist that this is unacceptable to him as a management policy/practice and that, while he is willing to respect Bill's wishes to retain the incapable employee (and do the best he can), he cannot accept criticism for that man's shortcomings which are largely responsible for Bernie's inability to perform the way he wants to and really can.

THE ESSENCE OF THIS APPROACH

Bernie is being firm and forthright: he is saying that he cannot continue in a job where he is blamed for a situation over which he is denied control by the very man who is blaming him. Bernie is also implying that he deserves greater respect from Bill and that he is not so afraid of losing his job that he will take the unfairness lying down.

B. Bernie can ask to meet with Bill and get the following points across:

- He likes his job and is honored to be working under Bill.
- He cannot, however, permit himself to be blamed for something which is not his fault.
- He likes working for the company and would prefer that it be under Bill, but if the situation doesn't change, he's going to apply for a transfer (through channels) to another department.

THE ESSENCE OF THIS APPROACH

Bernie lays it on the line and indicates — again fearlessly — that he will not continue in that department unless he is given all the authority he needs.

ADAPTING THESE SOLUTIONS TO YOUR OWN WORK

Whenever you get an assignment of responsibility from your boss check to make sure that you have all the necessary, concomitant authority for meeting the related accountability. Assume that you have that authority unless and until you are informed that you don't.

If that occurs, carefully document all the facts to substantiate that your ability to meet your accountability is being impaired by your relevant lack of authority; then carefully explain this to your boss.

If he persists, for whatever reason, in continuing to deny

you that authority, you've got to prevent him from blaming you for results which stem directly from that denial. If you don't he'll not really be considering you as a full manager and you'll lose your opportunities for shining as such in any event.

You're better off taking the bull by the horns earlier (rather than later), giving yourself a chance to re-establish your merit before it's too late.

SITUATION NUMBER 13 — The failure to use authority properly by your boss who bypasses you.

INCIDENT

Betty Lacey works for Charlie MacAdams. Charlie's a nice person to work for and is quite competent. He is, however, a bit impatient and often goes direct to Betty's assistants to ask them to do certain tasks for him. Betty finds this out only through supervision or when she asks one of her assistants to do something for her, with the reply that that assistant is currently doing something for Charlie.

ALTERNATE SOLUTIONS

A. Betty can go to Charlie and tell him that:

- She has discovered this practice.
- She knows Charlie means well.
- His engaging in that practice undermines her authority, confuses her assistants and makes it difficult for her to delegate her own assignments to them.
- She'd appreciate it if he asked only her to make the assignments.

THE ESSENCE OF THIS APPROACH

Betty tackles the problem directly though tactfully.

B. Betty can go to Charlie each time that she discovers that one of her assistants is working on an assignment direct from Charlie and say something like this to him:

"I've just found out that so-and-so is working on a task that you gave him directly. Do you want him to drop everything that I had previously assigned to him, or can your task wait until I can assign it in keeping with my carefully worked out schedule?"

THE ESSENCE OF THIS APPROACH

Betty brings the matter to Charlie's attention *each time,* emphasizing — each time — that Charlie is interfering with her work, but putting it to him subtly.

C. Betty can say to each of her assistants, on an individual basis and as the occasion warrants:

- Charlie is my boss and I respect and like him.
- He's a very competent, conscientious and successful manager and I am loyal to him.
- He does, however, sometimes get impatient to have a particular job done and comes direct to you.

- He doesn't intend for this to undermine my authority, but your fulfillment of his request interferes with my ability to plan properly and carry my plan out effectively.
- I want you to continue to show him all the respect he deserves, but I also want you to remember that I'm your only boss and that I'm the only one in this company who has the authority to assign tasks to you.
- Therefore, whenever Charlie asks you to do something for him, I want you to accept the work from Charlie and, as soon as he leaves your work area, to come to me and tell me about it. If I want you to do that job at that time I'll tell you so, but it will be because I agree with the timing even if I don't agree with the way in which the task was assigned.
- In every case I'll go to Charlie and explain to him why I asked you to do things my way.

THE ESSENCE OF THIS APPROACH

Betty clarifies her position forcefully with her assistants, makes possible their cooperation with her, emphasizes her authority over them and approaches the problem with Charlie on a more solid basis of having overruled his incorrect action.

ADAPTING THESE SOLUTIONS TO YOUR OWN WORK

Whenever your boss bypasses you to go direct to your assistants, asking them to do something for him, you must make sure to touch the following bases:

- Don't let your assistants accept such assignments without their firm awareness that they are not to do so without showing any disrespect for your boss.
- Be sure to point out to your boss *every* case of his bypassing you, with a respectful request that he desist from the practice.

SITUATION NUMBER 14 — The failure to use authority properly by your assistant who is your boss' favorite.

INCIDENT

Dave Nack has been with the company for many years. He has always gone out of his way to do favors of a personal nature for the superintendent, Eric Pace. Dave is one of Eric's favorites.

Between Dave and Eric, in the chain of command, is Dennis Quarles. Dave is in charge of the maintenance department and has five men reporting to him. Dennis has set up a very complete program of preventive and repair maintenance, to be managed by Dave, properly assigning tasks to his mechanics and other repairmen.

An important part of the program involves periodic fixed tours of inspection and testing by those men supervised by Dave. There has to be a weekly report on the dates, times and results of such tours, to be completed by Dave and given to Dennis.

Dave is quite careless about enforcing that program of inspection, although he is honest in his reporting, even when this shows his failure to insist that his men make the appropriate inspections.

Investigation has revealed to Dennis that there is no justification for the sloppy compliance with the program, and he has spoken to Dave about it. Dave's reply has been a good-natured effort to diminish the significance of such failure.

Dennis' reports to Eric on this have been met with the response that either Eric would take care of it (which he doesn't) or that Dennis is making too much of the occasional slipping of such a loyal and conscientious man.

ALTERNATE SOLUTIONS

A. Dennis can tell Dave that if the negligence continues, he — Dennis — will be forced to administer the preventive maintenance program himself and continue to complain about Dave to Eric.

THE ESSENCE OF THIS APPROACH

Dennis is, in effect, saying to both Dave and Eric: "I've tried to get Dave to manage properly and he can't or won't do what his job calls for. I've asked Eric to back me up in this and Eric has not done so. I am therefore functioning as though Dave were no longer available to me and am letting Eric know that I cannot and will not be held accountable for Dave's unprofitable impact on my department or for my less than excellent attention to the other assistants I have because I have to take the place of one of my assistants by myself.

B. Dennis can continue to supervise Dave, carefully document Dave's deficiencies — and the resulting damage to the company — and report these continually to Eric. Dennis refrains from doing Dave's work.

THE ESSENCE OF THIS APPROACH

Dennis is doing his best in an impossible situation, continues to function properly regarding his role as a manager over all of his assistants and puts the burden of accountability for Dave's failure to use his authority properly right where it belongs.

ADAPTING THESE SOLUTIONS TO YOUR OWN WORK

Your attitude toward all of your assistants must be that each of them has to do his job properly. If any one of them is a favorite of your boss, you must at first simply report the failing assistant for his failures, without making reference to your awareness of the favoritism. Do the best you can to get the favorite to perform properly, appeal to your boss for backup when appropriate and document carefully all pertinent actions, inactions and results.

If your boss won't back you up, do the best you can but protect yourself against unsubstantiatable and unwarranted criticism.

3

How to Handle Feelings of Unfair Treatment

In the following situations notice how the manager carefully analyzes the assertion of such treatment, by the complainant, to ascertain the accuracy or at least the tenability of the claim. Then, if there is any justification for the feeling, he assures the assistant that the cause will stop and sees to it that both it and the resulting unfairness come to an end, readily recognizable as such. If, however, the feeling is unjustified, the manager tries to make the employee aware of the incorrectness of his position and tries to reassure him of equal treatment being the rule and the practice. If he fails in this, he must insist that the man continue to do his work properly and refrain from telling anybody else what he thinks is a valid grievance.

SITUATION NUMBER 15 — Feelings of unfair treatment of an employee who complains of salary inequities.

INCIDENT

At salary review time, Dorothy Rabin recommended that Elaine Ullman, the office manager, be given a $200 salary increase for the next year. Dorothy made no recommendation for an increase for Florence Vaca. Florence was in charge of the mail room and reported directly to Dorothy.

When the first payroll period of the new year was ended, Dorothy's recommendations became known to many, as happens in most companies. Shortly thereafter Florence came to Dorothy and complained bitterly that:

- She'd been in the company as long as Elaine.
- She'd been a manager almost as long as Elaine.
- She was as hardworking and loyal as Elaine.
- Why didn't she also get an increase?

Dorothy's reasons, not yet disclosed to Florence, were:

- Elaine's management of her department was considerably more profitable than Florence's.
- Florence's job responsibilities were on a lower level of importance to the company than Elaine's.

ALTERNATE SOLUTIONS

A. Dorothy could simply say something like the following to Florence:

- I agree with everything you say to describe your work.
- But your position doesn't come under this year's policies regarding increases, and Elaine's does.
- Continue to do your usual good job and you'll get an increase in a year or two.

THE ESSENCE OF THIS APPROACH

Dorothy removes the problem from one of inferred unfairness to an accurate assessment of the differences between the two assistants in both job importance and company policy.

B. Dorothy could use the occasion for a more detailed communication to Florence about her role in the company by mentioning these points:

- Our company has a carefully worked out policy regarding the relationship between job duties and compensation.

- This policy has resulted in an arrangement of all jobs in our company in descending order of contribution to our success.
- Every job in that sequence is important to the company and, therefore, so is yours.
- Experience has shown, however, that we must reward good service in each department according to the contribution made by that department to overall profit.
- The job of office management in our company has far greater responsibilities than that of mail room supervisor.
- Therefore, when I am informed that I may recommend only certain salary increases, I must start with those jobs which are most important to the company.
- I have been given to understand that next year your job comes up for a recommendation for salary increase.
- You continue to do the same good job that you're doing now, perhaps succeeding in getting the mail distributed just a little more promptly than you were able to last year, and I'll recommend an increase for you as soon as that is authorized.

THE ESSENCE OF THIS APPROACH

You tell the basic truth and develop it, but make no promises that you may not be able to keep, trying to be as convincing as possible, praising wherever this is justified. Keep the decisions to positions and not to individuals.

ADAPTING THESE SOLUTIONS TO YOUR OWN WORK

Whenever one of your employees gives indication of dissatisfaction with his compensation, as compared with that of someone else in the company, make sure to touch at least the following bases:

- Your decision regarding increasing one salary and not another was based on purely organizational reasons, not on personalities.

- Find the simplest and most convincing explanation of why one got the increase and the other didn't.
- Make sure that the grieving employee understands your reasoning and try to get him to accept it, but don't be too much concerned if he *doesn't* accept it.
- Praise wherever you can, encourage improvement in areas related to the meriting of an increase and hold out whatever promise you can — but don't commit yourself to any promise you may not be able to keep.

SITUATION NUMBER 16 — Feelings of unfair treatment of the manager who feels his budget is too low.

INCIDENT

Leo Rackoff is in charge of company office services. His boss is Ralph Yaeger. When Ralph has given Leo his budget for the next fiscal year, in the preparation of which Leo — like all other department heads — had participated, Leo comes to Ralph to complain. He says that his request for a budget provision for an additional mailroom clerk was turned down, leading to two elements of dissatisfaction for him:

- He needs that additional clerk.
- The EDP department manager had also requested an additional clerk, and that request had been granted because Ralph favors the EDP department over the office services department.

ALTERNATE SOLUTIONS

A. Where it is true, Ralph says that he had put Leo's request in with approval, but that it had been turned down for valid reasons of work load, which Ralph agrees with and is prepared to explain to Leo. This means that Leo must completely disabuse himself of the claim of unfair treatment. Ralph is prepared to go over with Leo how the latter can effectively run his services without that extra clerk.

THE ESSENCE OF THIS APPROACH

Ralph indicates that he had supported Leo until he —
Ralph — was convinced that the request should be denied for
company reasons. Ralph urges Leo to stop thinking that anyone has treated him unfairly and offers to help Leo solve the
problem he has or thinks he has.

B. Where Ralph has himself turned down Leo's request —
because Ralph had made a careful analysis leading to the conclusion that the request was not justified at that time — Ralph
can talk to Leo along these lines:

- Leo's request at this time was inconsistent with the overall budget needs of both Ralph's entire section and the
  company as a whole, which is why Ralph turned it down.
- Leo's claim that he was being treated unfairly was entirely unfounded and Ralph resents Leo's entertaining such
  thoughts. Furthermore, Leo is not to express that false
  sentiment to anyone.
- Ralph will work with Leo to solve any problems Leo
  thinks will stem from his inability to perform adequately
  without the additional clerk.

THE ESSENCE OF THIS APPROACH

Ralph assumes full responsibility for the decision, offers to
help Leo solve his problems and focuses most of his attention
on the unjustified complaint of unfair treatment.

ADAPTING THESE SOLUTIONS TO YOUR OWN WORK

When you get a budget request from one of your assistants, analyze it very carefully. As soon as possible, and before
you pass the budget on up to your boss, let your assistant know
what decision *you've* reached regarding his request.

If *your* decision has been to turn him down, explain to him
why at that time. If you have endorsed his request and it has
been turned down above you, tell him that you endorse that
decision, using the reasons given to you.

Whenever the decision is adverse to your assistant's feelings, handle it this way:

- Get out of the way first any assertion or implication by him that he is being treated unfairly by you or anyone else. Don't let him get away with it: insist that he not express that unjustified feeling to anyone else.
- Offer to help him with his problem if it's real. If it's only believed (by him) to be a problem, disabuse him of that idea.

SITUATION NUMBER 17 — Feelings of unfair treatment of the technician who objects to his paperwork load.

INCIDENT

Dick Abbott is chief estimator in the division. He is accountable to Norm Yancy. Dick has fallen behind in meeting his schedule of completing estimates for the last few months. Norm has pointed this out to Dick previously; Dick's response was simply that he'd try to do better, resisting Norm's invitation to explain why Dick had failed to keep up.

Now Norm calls Dick in and says that the backlog has not only continued but has become quite serious. Dick complains that Norm's criticism is unfair because:

- Norm has given Dick a very heavy schedule, which Dick could accomplish if he were given the opportunity to enforce it.
- The reason he hasn't been able to supervise his technicians' work in such a way as to assure meeting the schedule is that Dick has had too much paperwork, the completion of which prevented him from doing his proper job of managing his technicians.

ALTERNATE SOLUTIONS

A. Norm analyzes the paperwork situation in order to find out whether Dick's assertion is correct. If it is, he assures Dick that the load will be reduced, thus allowing Dick to perform properly. Norm also expresses his regret at having jumped to a wrong conclusion.

THE ESSENCE OF THIS APPROACH

Norm goes immediately to the verities of Dick's claim and, if Dick was right, apologizes for his unjustified assessment and takes steps to make it possible for Dick to do his job well.

B. Norm asks Dick why he didn't raise the question of paperwork before, the idea being that Norm wants to arrive at the real explanation of Dick's continued failure to meet the schedule.

Norm then cautions Dick that in future he is to raise his objections at the times that they are, in his opinion, valid, not waiting until a later time. Norm is then in a position to analyze the problem and decide whether its solution lies in diminishing unjustified paperwork or in Dick's paying proper attention to *every* element of his duties.

THE ESSENCE OF THIS APPROACH

Norm isolates the various problems represented by Dick's position or attitude. Where Dick has failed to complain previously about the paperwork and raises the issue only the last time he is criticized for not meeting schedules, he lays himself open to the charge that he had thought of an excuse only when he felt his back was against the wall. After that is gotten out of the way Norm is ready to tackle the major problem: meeting the schedule without any unjustified accusations of unfair treatment.

C. Norm can come to the conclusion that the paperwork load is necessary exactly as it is. If this is so, Norm must tell Dick so and try to convince him of that fact. Whether he can "sell" Dick on it or not, he must point out that Dick must pay equal attention to all of his duties rather than favor those which he likes. Here, too, Norm must emphasize to Dick that his unjustified charge of unfair treatment must neither interfere with his work nor be bruited about.

THE ESSENCE OF THIS APPROACH

Norm re-emphasizes to Dick the total nature of his job, the importance of doing all of it well and the need to avoid feeling or saying that he has been treated unfairly when he hasn't been.

ADAPTING THESE SOLUTIONS TO YOUR OWN WORK

There is a strong tendency on the part of a number of assistants to dislike paperwork and prefer to do what their technical abilities call for. You must, of course, make sure never to put so much of a load on any assistant — whether paperwork or otherwise — that he can't really pay the right attention to every facet of his work. Once you know that you have not made that mistake, try to explain to your assistant that he is incorrectly assessing the situation, that he must meet all of his duties equally and that he must not continue to feel or say that he has been unfairly treated.

SITUATION NUMBER 18 — Feelings of unfair treatment of supervisor who wasn't promoted.

INCIDENT

Harvey Umans had been a supervisor in the company for ten years. Paul Jackson had been one for only four years. Both reported to Ed Nagy.

A vacancy occurred in another department, also reporting to Ed, on a higher level than the one occupied by both Harvey and Paul. Ed recommended to his boss that Paul be promoted to that vacancy and his recommendation was accepted. Ed notified Paul of his new job.

When Harvey learned of this he came to see Ed and bitterly complained that he should have gotten the job because he's been around longer than Paul and was better qualified for the job than Paul. He also said that his failure to get the upgrading was unfair treatment.

ALTERNATE SOLUTIONS

A. Ed can tell Harvey that he — Harvey — is mistaken about who is better qualified than whom, that he — Ed — is the only judge of that, that longevity in itself is not the prevailing factor (although it is taken into consideration) and that Harvey is acting in a less than mature and loyal way in raising the question of unfairness before getting all the facts.

THE ESSENCE OF THIS APPROACH

Ed affirms his own right to make this kind of judgment, discounts longevity as the major or only cause for promotion and chides Harvey for jumping to conclusions.

B. Ed can explain to Harvey that:

- Ed appreciates all that Harvey has done for the company.
- Ed took into consideration Harvey's longevity.
- All things considered, Ed felt that Paul was better qualified for that promotion, giving the reasons for this conclusion.
- Harvey's chance will come.
- Under no circumstances can Ed tolerate the kind of invalid claim of unfair treatment.

THE ESSENCE OF THIS APPROACH

Ed tries *first* to "sell" Harvey on Ed's position on the subject. Then Ed tries to raise Harvey's morale. Finally, Ed firmly clarifies his stand against unjustified charges of unfairness.

ADAPTING THESE SOLUTIONS TO YOUR OWN WORK

It might be well to talk to a longer-employed assistant before promoting someone else, to try to explain to him why the promotion is being made as planned and the real effect of this on him. If the assistant then insists that he has been treated unfairly, you can take your firm stand against that feeling before it has a chance to spread; also, you can then caution the assistant not to tell anyone his unjustified charge of unfair treatment.

SITUATION NUMBER 19 — Feelings of unfair treatment of a manager who feels his office was too small.

INCIDENT

Joe MacDonald is a department head, and so is Gabe Zane. Both of them work under Howard Talbot.

Joe's office is in the same building as the assistants who report to him, while Gabe's is in the main enclave of offices. Howard had to enlarge some of the offices and rearrange others in order to adjust to the addition of new people and new responsibilities. Gabe's was one of those scheduled to be enlarged; nothing was to be done in the other building in that regard.

Joe came to see Howard and complained that:

- He needed more space in his office too.
- His job was just as important as Gabe's and he feared that his assistants would interpret the change as an enhancement of Gabe and a diminishing of Joe.
- Joe felt that the situation dealt with him unfairly.

There was no way that Howard could conveniently increase the size of any office in Joe's building.

ALTERNATE SOLUTIONS

A. Howard could assure Joe that there was no alternative to the new setup and that no unfairness was involved. He promised Joe that he would do everything in his power to create the impression that Joe's job was just as important as Gabe's despite the office sizes.

THE ESSENCE OF THIS APPROACH

Howard tries to soothe Joe's feelings without taking up too much time and without making a great fuss about it.

B. Howard can show Joe the building plans and try to convince him that the changes in the new building must be made as planned. He can also emphasize that it's absolutely essential for

Joe to stay in the building where he now is (because of the necessary proximity to his men), a location which doesn't presently lend itself to the enlargement of offices.

THE ESSENCE OF THIS APPROACH

Howard takes a little more time and effort in order to convince Joe that no unfairness is intended and that the situation is irremediable.

C. Howard can tell Joe that he will take the following steps to overcome any possible misinterpretation of the reasons for the planned difference in office sizes:

- Howard will send out a notice to all management and salaried employees explaining the new office setup.
- In it he will explain the reasons for the differences in size.
- He will then call a meeting of all of the assistants to both Joe and Gabe, the latter two also being present, at which he will tactfully but firmly convey the true impression that the difference in size between the two offices has no relation to the relative importance of the departments in question.

Howard must also insist that Joe admit wholeheartedly that there is no unfairness in the decision to enlarge only Gabe's office as opposed to Joe's.

THE ESSENCE OF THIS APPROACH

Howard tries to help Joe overcome his feeling by direct appeal to the employees whose opinion Joe fears. In exchange, however, Joe must rid himself of his unjustified feelings of unfairness.

ADAPTING THESE SOLUTIONS TO YOUR OWN WORK

Whenever you plan to make a change in physical layouts which might be misinterpreted as creating different levels of prestige, it's wise to call all parties involved in, individually or in groups, in order to try to prevent the feeling of unfairness. If, after that, the feeling still persists you can be very firm about the lack of justification.

4

How to Handle Problems With Fellow Managers

In the following situations notice how important it is for each manager to deal with his fellow managers in a way designed to assure desirable company profit simultaneously making each manager personally more successful and happier on the job. Notice that the key to this cooperation is an open mind, a readiness to understand the other's viewpoint, a sincere desire to meet him half way and — above all — effective mutual communications.

SITUATION NUMBER 20 — Problems with fellow managers where the credit manager is too strict on sales.

INCIDENT

Ken Backman is the sales manager. Lloyd Cade is the credit manager. Ken's salesmen are for the most part a very conscientious and capable group. They are constantly calling on the right mix of prospects and customers for the right mix of company products. They consistently meet minimum acceptable quotas and many frequently exceed them.

Ken's men have been reporting to him that many of their customers are complaining that they will be forced to buy from the competition if the credit department continues to give them a hard time. Ken has spot-checked among his more reliable customers and has confirmed the salesmen's reports.

ALTERNATE SOLUTIONS

A. Ken can ask the credit manager to discuss the matter and find out why so many customers are complaining that the company's credit policies and practices are too harsh. If he cannot agree with the wisdom of Lloyd's insistence on continuing that severity, he asks Lloyd to accompany him to the general manager for a ruling.

THE ESSENCE OF THIS APPROACH

Ken makes an effort to go through proper channels at the same time that he tries to stick up for his men and his customers.

B. Ken can make a careful study of the entire set of customer complaints. He then analyzes them to see in which cases he believes the credit manager is being overly zealous. He carefully studies the company's credit policies and practices; then he tries to get the credit manager to interpret these a bit more liberally in the interest of greater dollar sales volume and retention of good customers.

THE ESSENCE OF THIS APPROACH

Ken is armed with hard facts. Even then he asks the other manager to be reasonable rather than insisting on what he may have discovered to be a wiser interpretation than the one being administered. He can still, of course, embrace the appeal procedure if necessary.

C. Ken can analyze the history of sales lost by the company over the last few years and estimate how many of these — as well as the total sales volume involved — were lost (or not renewed) because of credit policies and practices which were excessive for the protection of the company. He also makes an analysis of the relative loss to the company of accounts receivable outstanding versus profit from sales lost because of the desire to keep that amount low.

Ken can then sit down with Lloyd and discuss the matter as follows:

- Ken recognizes and appreciates Lloyd's sincere desire to do his job well.
- Ken also knows that Lloyd is a reasonable man, flexible and objective.
- Here are the facts about profit and loss related to the company's sales vis-à-vis credit.
- Can't we work something out between us, for the good of the company, so that you can continue to protect the company's money values at the same time that you help promote profitable sales?

THE ESSENCE OF THIS APPROACH

Ken flatters Lloyd (deservedly) and then presents him with persuasive arguments. Finally, he appeals to Lloyd to temper his justified interest in his own responsibility with an awareness of the equal contribution to be made by certain sales governed by more realistic credit practices.

ADAPTING THESE SOLUTIONS TO YOUR OWN WORK

The battles between a salesman (and therefore his sales manager) and the credit department are numerous. The salesman — especially if his compensation is geared to his dollar volume in sales — is interested in selling as much as he can all the time. The credit manager, on the other hand, is just as avid to keep accounts receivable outstanding and losses from bad accounts to the barest possible minimum.

The credit manager, then, has a tendency to enforce rigidly the company's policies and procedures in this connection and even to give them the strictest possible interpretation.

Each of these two department heads is doing what he considers best for the company, but the two of them together must try to arrive at a compromise which meets *all* of the following conditions:

- Accounts receivable which exceed minimum acceptable levels — maximum days outstanding — for profitable, reliable customers may have to be negotiated between sales and credit to determine whether an exception to the rule would result in greater or less profit to the company.

- Salesmen must be cautioned not to sell at any particular time to accounts which must appropriately be turned down because their credit position warrants this from an overall company standpoint.

And the sales manager must see to it that his salesmen are kept informed of such situations in advance of their sales effort.

Above all, the two department heads must establish and maintain a continuing relationship of mutual communication and understanding.

SITUATION NUMBER 21 — Problems with fellow managers where the next flow department manager blames you for deadline failure.

INCIDENT

Lou Dade is in charge of purchasing raw materials. Mac Early handles telephone orders from customers. When a customer phones an order in, Mac's people are supposed to check the levels of inventory for the items requested before accepting the order. If a particular item is not listed as available — or to be available — at the time that a customer wants delivery, Mac's men must ask the customer to hold a moment (or say they'll call him back right away) while they check with Lou's clerks on the availability.

On some occasions when Mac's people haven't checked sufficiently, this results in embarrassing if not unprofitable relations with the customers involved. On other occasions, Lou's people haven't seen to it that materials were available when they had said they would be.

Lou and Mac blame each other for the carelessness and negligence in question.

ALTERNATE SOLUTIONS

A. Either Lou or Mac must take the initiative to sit down with the other and discuss the situation. An effort must be made by both of them to be calm, objective and cooperative. Both must recognize that each of them must be motivated only by what's best for the company. Neither of them must be defensive about his own department.

At this meeting an effort must be made to arrive at the closest possible assessment of the facts and steps must be resolved on which to prevent recurrences.

Each of them must then go back to his men, tell them firmly how they must approach the matter and supervise them more carefully in order to prevent repetitions of the incidents.

THE ESSENCE OF THIS APPROACH

- Each department head takes the initiative where appropriate.
- A sincere effort is made to arrive at the facts.
- The meeting is held in a spirit of compromise and cooperation.
- Each one tries thereafter to see to it that his men comply.

B. If such a meeting is thwarted by the other department head, or when held, doesn't yield positive results, either one of them (or each of them) can:

- Request the other to accompany him to their joint boss, indicating (if the other refuses) that he will go anyway.
- Lay the facts and firm opinions before the third party and ask for his assessment and judgment, to be followed by a conclusive ruling.

THE ESSENCE OF THIS APPROACH

Normal appeal procedures are followed when necessary.

C. The company can establish, communicate and enforce a new procedure for handling such flow like this:

- Whenever a telephone order taker consults the records or an authorized purchasing department employee for material availability, a copy of the order should immediately be passed on to Lou or his designee.
- Meanwhile Mac's people process the order.

- Lou or his designee must immediately check the order to make sure that it conforms to actual availability.

THE ESSENCE OF THIS APPROACH

The purchasing people have an immediate opportunity to double-check on the accuracy of the other department's judgments, thus allowing for prompt correction where necessary, before too much harm has been done.

ADAPTING THESE SOLUTIONS TO YOUR OWN WORK

In most management obligations the ability of one manager to meet his own responsibilities depends in large measure on the way in which one or more other managers meet theirs. The emphasis is on smooth, continuing, profitable flow of results from one department to another.

Any one manager who discovers that he can't meet his own needs because he isn't getting the proper flow from another manager should immediately take the initiative to:

- Investigate and ascertain the facts.
- Discuss them with the other manager(s).
- Jointly try to resolve the problem.
- Appeal to a joint immediate superior when necessary.

SITUATION NUMBER 22 — Problems with fellow managers where the personnel manager hires a man for you without consulting you.

INCIDENT

Walt Yancy is a superintendent in the manufacturing division. He has filled out and sent to Marty Fader, the personnel manager, a requisition for a specific type of worker needed by one of Walt's foremen.

Company policy and procedure is that Marty's recruiters engage in preliminary screening and make recommendations to the requisitioner, but do not make the hiring decision. When the requisitioner approves a candidate recommended by personnel and so communicates to them, they then engage in the hiring process.

In this particular case one of Marty's men told a candidate for the position requested by Walt that he was satisfactory and had been hired. The man then presented himself to Walt's foreman with papers which indicated that fact.

The foreman immediately reported this to Walt, while asking the candidate/hiree to wait a moment.

ALTERNATE SOLUTIONS

A. Walt can interview the man along with his foreman, see whether he is really acceptable and, if he is, confirm the hiring — in no way, of course, letting on to the man what the problem was. If the man is not acceptable, the foreman tells him so, expressing his regret over the misunderstanding and sending him back to personnel for possible reassignment.

In either case, after the fact, Walt asks Marty to be more careful in future and see to it that his people don't do the same thing again.

THE ESSENCE OF THIS APPROACH

Walt tries to salvage the situation and then asks Marty to prevent its recurrence.

B. Walt can ask the foreman to tell the man to wait a moment. Walt then goes to Marty and tells him what has happened and why he objects to it. Walt suggests that he send the man back to Marty and let Marty straighten out both the candidate/hiree and (not in the latter's presence) his man who made the mistake.

Walt then asks Marty to have the new man rescreened and sent back to him (if feasible) if he is to be reconsidered, such man being in full possession of the understanding that the second time he goes to the foreman it is with the proper awareness of his position.

THE ESSENCE OF THIS APPROACH

Walt nips the problem in the bud at once, reducing to the barest possible minimum any delay in the new man's understanding of his status and throwing the burden of the solution where it belongs.

ADAPTING THESE SOLUTIONS TO YOUR OWN WORK

Unless it is contrary to established company policy and procedure, the best kind of relationship between personnel and operations with regard to hiring is this:

- Operations completes and sends to personnel a properly filled out form requesting personnel to recruit for a stated position, with a specified number of vacancies and pursuant to a well understood set of specifications.
- Personnel recruits and engages in preliminary screening, rejecting those who they feel don't qualify at all and referring the others to operations.
- If operations accepts a candidate, he is taken to personnel for hire processing.

SITUATION NUMBER 23 — Problems with fellow managers where you don't get the proper components from the flow manager preceding your processing.

INCIDENT

Nick Gador's department makes up the first weldment in the manufacturing process. These weldments are then scheduled to move directly into Oscar Imerman's bay for the next step.

The production control manager has engineered the flow in such a way that Oscar should receive a steady movement of those weldments into his section so that he can do with them on time what's called for by the schedule.

Lately, Oscar's foremen have told him that there have been several occasions when those weldments are not available on schedule, resulting in down time until the flow resumes.

ALTERNATE SOLUTIONS

A. Oscar can go to Nick and ask him to make sure that those weldments flow according to schedule or, whenever it turns out that this is going to be impossible, to let Oscar know that fact well in advance so that he — Oscar — can plan around it.

THE ESSENCE OF THIS APPROACH

Oscar seeks a solution which promotes cooperation and good feeling, at the same time that it seeks to prevent Oscar from suffering from situations which Nick may, perhaps, not be able to control.

B. Oscar can document every occasion when he doesn't receive his components at all or on time. He can then make periodic reports to the production control manager indicating why he — Oscar — can't meet his own schedules.

THE ESSENCE OF THIS APPROACH

Oscar assumes that Nick is doing the best he can and does nothing to imply a criticism of the latter. He protects himself from criticism and leaves remedial action to production control.

C. Oscar asks Nick what the problem is and suggests that the two of them go and see the production control manager to try to get at the root of the problem and solve it for the benefit of all, including, of course, the company.

THE ESSENCE OF THIS APPROACH

Oscar offers to cooperate with Nick and help solve whatever problem exists by the two of them going to the one man who should be able to help them.

ADAPTING THESE SOLUTIONS TO YOUR OWN WORK

When your department is not getting the flow from a preceding one which is essential to your ability to keep up to production schedules, try first to find out the cause. In the process, avoid creating an impression of criticism. Then be ready to help in every way possible, but always be ready to protect yourself against criticism for not meeting schedules where it's beyond your control.

SITUATION NUMBER 24 — Problems with fellow managers where the other manager doesn't enforce the same rules as you do.

INCIDENT

Vance Haines is responsible for a production area which contains flammable materials. Steve Kagan manages a different area, with less flammable items. The company rule is the same for both of them: no smoking is permitted at work stations; employees must go to specified smoking areas if they wish to indulge and, of course, they can do this only during authorized breaks.

Vance's foremen complain to him that their respective employees strongly object to his efforts to enforce the rule, saying that they don't see why they have to be deprived of the right to smoke when Steve's people can be seen smoking at their work stations all the time.

ALTERNATE SOLUTIONS

A. Vance can tell his foremen to handle the situation as follows:

- Every time that one of the workers smokes at his work station, the foreman must know it.

- The foreman must then, in polite but firm language, ask the worker to stop smoking and explain that it's the rule, which he intends to enforce consistently.

- If a worker complains that Steve's people are permitted to smoke at their work stations, and goes on to indicate things like its unfairness or officiousness, the foreman is simply to say: I have no comment about anyone else's department. I am accountable to Vance for how I run my department and to him only. He and I are both dedicated to enforcing all company rules consistently.

THE ESSENCE OF THIS APPROACH

The foreman meets the violation calmly but consistently and firmly, insisting that the rule must be observed. When a worker mentions the fact that that same rule is being violated elsewhere, the foreman doesn't rise to the provocation and handles the situation only as it affects his own bailiwick. He neither follows nor criticizes the offending department.

B. Vance can go to Steve and tell him what's happening. He can then tell Steve that he — Vance — is dedicated to following the rule, and that if it is true that Steve's foremen aren't, this is making it difficult for Vance to enforce it and also tends to anger his foremen's workers unjustifiably.

If Steve fails to cooperate, Vance must follow normal appeal procedures to their joint boss.

THE ESSENCE OF THIS APPROACH

Vance tries to eliminate the cause of the problem, thus improving the relationship between his foremen and their respective workers.

ADAPTING THESE SOLUTIONS TO YOUR OWN WORK

When your company establishes a rule for you, you should voice any objections you have to that rule as soon as such objections become obvious to you. If, however, the rule still stands, you must enforce it and you must insist that your assistants enforce it too.

If another department is less strict about the enforcement of that rule, and your people throw that up to you when you try to enforce it, you must be careful not to criticize the other department. As a matter of fact, you're better off pleading ignorance of their assertions and handling the enforcement with only the barest minimum of mention of the other department.

If, however, the situation becomes increasingly difficult, you should try first to persuade the other manager to help you out of the difficulty by enforcing the rule equally. If he doesn't respond favorably, you should tell him that you'd like the two of you to put the matter before your joint boss for him to settle.

5

How to Handle
The New Hire

In the following situations notice how important it is to pay very careful attention to early indications that he may not be adjusting satisfactorily to his new job or may be discontented with or in it. The earlier you become aware of a problem or potential problem with a new employee, the more easily you can cope with it. You can either guide him into overcoming whatever the difficulty is, or you can come to the conclusion that you made an unwise choice and separate him before that becomes too painful or costly.

SITUATION NUMBER 25 — The new hire who's always talking about better conditions in his last place.

INCIDENT

Rita Laden was hired about three weeks ago to be in charge of the switchboard, reporting to Susan O'Brien, the office manager. Rita is competent and knowledgeable. She deals with the other switchboard operators in fine managerial style. The only trouble is that Rita is always sounding off to anyone who will listen to her — including her own switchboard operators — about the inferiority of her present situation (as compared to her

75

last place) regarding the kind of board, the policies and procedures for using the telephone, the size and arrangement of the reception area (where the board is located), the working hours and the food in the lunch room.

Not only has Susan heard Rita doing this in her presence, but a number of employees have come to Susan to complain about the effect this is having on those who are loyal to the company and quite happy with their working conditions. These complainers include Rita's own assistants.

ALTERNATE SOLUTIONS

A.   Susan can ask Rita to sit down with her privately, so that no one will suspect the nature of the talk, and develop the following ideas with her:

- Susan knows for a fact that Rita has been complaining about a number of things here, comparing them unfavorably with her last place of work.
- Susan wants Rita to understand that if there are any items in this company which Rita thinks should be improved, she is to come to Susan directly with her suggestions, but without reference to her last place.
- Susan will do everything possible to remedy any shortcomings in the company indicated by Rita, to the extent possible.
- Regardless of anything that Susan can or cannot do in that connection, it is bad for Rita — and the company — to be and have the reputation of being a griper.
- She undermines her own position by being a griper.

THE ESSENCE OF THIS APPROACH

Susan tries to impress Rita with the proper avenue of complaint and with the damage Rita is doing herself by griping about this company, especially in contrast with her former company.

B.   Susan can ask those who report to her on Rita's griping to disregard it, thanking them for telling her about it. She can then increase her supervision of Rita to see whether she is really as suitable for the job as she seemed to be when she was hired.

If it turns out that she really isn't a superior manager, Susan can then ask the personnel department to start looking for Rita's replacement, both within the company and without.

Then, as soon as Susan has found someone suited for the job she can give Rita notice of separation on the grounds of general failure to meet the expectations surrounding her having been hired.

THE ESSENCE OF THIS APPROACH

It has generally been found that a manager who doesn't understand the importance of loyalty to the company is generally deficient in other aspects of management. It then hardly pays to try to salvage such an individual when he or she has been with the company such a short time. It's wiser to admit a mistake and start all over again with someone else.

ADAPTING THESE SOLUTIONS TO YOUR OWN WORK

As soon as you learn that a new hire under your control is going about complaining about his job or the company, especially in contrast with his former place of work, you had better give careful thought to the real reasons for the complaining:

- Is it only a cover-up for a recognized inability to do the job?
- Are there any legitimate complaints which should be heeded? At the same time the new hire should be advised about the wrong and right channels of making suggestions for improvement.
- Is a caution against unwise talk all that is needed or is the new hire really not suited for the job?

SITUATION NUMBER 26 — The new hire whose appearance clashes with company standards.

INCIDENT

Adolph Packer had been interviewed by his prospective boss, Ben Quill, for a job on the main floor of the company office. At that time Adolph had been neatly and conservatively attired and well groomed, except for perhaps excessively long sideburns —

at least Ben thought them excessively long because they called Ben's attention to themselves in distraction from Adolph the person.

Adolph had all the qualifications for the job, however, and seemed enthusiastic about accepting it, and Ben had had difficulty filling it.

Several weeks after Adolph started working there, Ben began to notice a steady change in Adolph's appearance, in the direction of ever-longer hair (beginning to look unkempt), an unusual type of moustache and a beard. (Adolph was twenty-four years old, short and slight.) Adolph also took to wearing a rather seedy-looking sweater and jeans carefully prepared to look old and nonconformist. His work, however, didn't suffer.

Ben noticed that a few other employees on the main floor were beginning to approach Adolph's new style of dress and grooming in their own appearance. Several customers had also remarked rather unfavorably to Ben on Adolph's appearance.

The company's policy simply said that employees were expected to dress and groom themselves with neatness and dignity, in keeping with the company's need to present that kind of image to the many visitors who frequently came to the main floor.

ALTERNATE SOLUTIONS

A. Ben can call Adolph in and say to him:

- You seem to be working out all right in your new job.
- I assume you're happy here.
- Your work calls for you to be stationed on the main floor.
- Many important visitors have asked me why one of our employees doesn't present the appearance they deem dignified.
- Would it cause you too much unhappiness if you conformed to our company standards?

THE ESSENCE OF THIS APPROACH

Ben first praises Adolph. He then gently points out the possible trouble that Adolph could unwittingly cause the company and appeals to his good sense and fairness.

B. Ben could move Adolph down to the company basement

to do his work where customers and other important suppliers and visitors don't go.

THE ESSENCE OF THIS APPROACH

Adolph can continue to give in to his preferences of dress and grooming and Ben would not be put into the embarrassing position of bringing up a purely personal matter.

C. Ben could tell Adolph that he has manifested a style of dress and grooming quite different from what he showed when he was hired, and that the new appearance was contrary to company standards. He could then tell Adolph that this was interfering with the desirable image the company wanted to maintain vis-à-vis outsiders, as well as having an unsalutary effect on other employees.

He could then tell Adolph that he will have to conform to company standards.

THE ESSENCE OF THIS APPROACH

Ben tries to make Adolph realize that he has exhibited an attitude considerably different from the one which contributed to his being hired. He then goes on to point out that Adolph must conform to company standards.

D. Ben can sit down with Adolph and try to get him to:

- Recognize that he has changed his habits since he was hired.
- See that the change was not for the better.
- Understand why the company has the standards it has.
- Agree to change back to his previous appearance.

THE ESSENCE OF THIS APPROACH

Ben tries to be reasonable throughout and appeals to Adolph's logic.

ADAPTING THESE SOLUTIONS TO YOUR OWN WORK

Despite any trend in court decisions which seem to make it difficult for companies to enforce its rules on appearance, you have to try to establish, communicate and enforce those reasonable standards which you feel important to your company. Set the standards in such a way that there is a strong chance that they will be considered reasonable if a challenge is ever raised about them.

Be very careful in screening candidates for vacant jobs. You might be challenged in a court if you refused to hire someone for unusual appearance, but if a candidate demonstrates tendencies of any kind which seem not to conform to your standards, it's best not to hire him. Be careful not to give any indication that appearance had anything to do with your decision.

The moment a new hire begins to show an undesirable change in appearance, try to persuade him not to go that route. If that doesn't work, either put him somewhere that his undesirable appearance won't harm the company or see whether his general attitude toward all company standards doesn't justify separation.

SITUATION NUMBER 27 — The new hire who has had no experience in his new work.

INCIDENT

Desmond Sabin had been an industrial foreman in a trucking company for many years. The company was moving its operations out of the state and Desmond couldn't go with them if he wanted to keep his family happy. That's why Desmond looked for another job, with his company's full knowledge and approval.

Eli Wagner was superintendent of a metal processing plant, in need of a foreman for one of the various metal departments. Eli's newspaper ad brought Desmond to the company and the personnel department thought it worth Eli's while to see him. Eli agreed. Even though Desmond had no knowledge of metals he had all the other qualities he was looking for in a good foreman — and Eli had no existing employee whose knowledge of metals made up for his lack of qualifications for being an effective foreman.

Eli hired Desmond. The immediate problem was what to do about Desmond's lack of metal knowledge.

ALTERNATE SOLUTIONS

A. Eli could make do the best he could without a foreman for that department, using another foreman to double up, bolstered by Eli himself. Meanwhile, Eli could submit Desmond to an intensive training program in metals knowledge.

THE ESSENCE OF THIS APPROACH

The department is run fairly effectively without Desmond, while his education is thereby accelerated.

B. Eli could assign the best worker in the department as an adviser to Desmond. Eli would make provision for that worker's load to be carried by someone else and sit down with both Desmond and the worker to set up a program along these lines:

- Desmond is to start at once as foreman.
- Eli will personally introduce him to all the men in his new department, emphasizing that he's a good supervisor, has full authority at once, will soon know the metals involved and is being helped by the worker.
- The worker is to concentrate on advising Desmond, but he is to have no authority over the men.
- Desmond will learn the metals from the worker as he — Desmond — goes along exercising normal foremanship duties.
- In that process, as Desmond comes across a problem involving the knowledge of metals, as distinguished from management concepts, he can lean on the worker.
- Whenever the time can be spared, the worker will increase Desmond's knowledge of the metals.

THE ESSENCE OF THIS APPROACH

Desmond begins at once to fill the foremanship need. Also, he learns on the job. In a pinch, he can always shore up his own lack of metals knowledge from the worker assigned to him for that purpose.

C. Eli could have one of the other foreman take on two

departments, his own and the new one. Desmond can be assigned
to him as assistant to the foreman, with no authority of his own.
When the other foreman must be in his own department he can
give Desmond temporary authority over the new one, urging
Desmond to call on him in an emergency. The other foreman
trains Desmond until it is no longer necessary, at which point
Desmond is made full foreman.

THE ESSENCE OF THIS APPROACH

There is a maximum, effective coverage of both departments,
obeying the principle of one man — one boss, while materials
training is going on.

ADAPTING THESE SOLUTIONS TO YOUR OWN WORK

Try always to have one worker or more who is so well developed by you that he can be moved into vacant foremanship
jobs. Failing in this, don't be so under strength in foremanship
coverage that you can't effectively spread one foreman over two
departments when necessary; also, plan your own work in such
a way that you can easily pinch hit as a foreman backup without
hurting the rest of your responsibilities.

When you need a new foreman, then, his lack of knowledge
of your materials — or any other specific in your company different from his own past experience — will not present a difficult
problem.

SITUATION NUMBER 28 — The new hire who seems indiffer-
ent to company profit objectives.

INCIDENT

Glen Badger is the new dispatcher. The traffic manager is
Ike Caffrey. Glen's job calls for him to receive requests for
making company vehicles and/or commercial carrier vehicles
available for use in connection with the company's shipping
program.

Ike has been studying the Controller's reports, along with
Glen's and his own. He finds that there are many deadhead trips

where a company vehicle delivers finished materials from the plant to the customer and comes back empty. He also finds that there are a number of occasions when the company is charged for common carrier freight from suppliers of raw materials in locations en route to the company's own customers. Finally, he discovers that there are a number of occasions when Glen has engaged common carriers when the company's own vehicles would have been available.

ALTERNATE SOLUTIONS

A. Ike can ask Glen to show him the forms and guidelines he uses in assigning vehicles for runs, as well as in deciding whether to use a company vehicle as distinguished from one engaged from a common carrier. Ike can also ask to see the notices Glen receives from the shipping department as well as the requests for pickups received from the purchasing department.

If these are in any way to blame for Glen's seeming indifference to company profit, then Ike can take the necessary steps to remedy the causes.

THE ESSENCE OF THIS APPROACH

Ike investigates causes before assuming an attitude of indifference on the part of the new hire.

B. Ike can spend a few days sitting with Glen in the minute-by-minute performance of his duties. He would let Glen do exactly what he normally does, but he would examine all documents and ask the reasons for all relevant decisions.

At the end of that time Ike would be in a good position to know why Glen makes the decisions he does and what is the real reason for the seeming indifference to profits: poor procedures and forms stemming from others; Glen's carelessness or indifference; or Glen's need for more training or inability to do the job.

THE ESSENCE OF THIS APPROACH

Ike personally investigates and sees first-hand what the situation is. He can then take the corrective steps indicated.

C. Ike can review all the existing procedures and forms related to those decisions. He makes sure that they are in the condition he wants.

He then calls together the proper people from receiving, shipping and dispatch (Glen) to review with them how he wants the flow of communications to operate.

Once he's sure they all understand this, he checks very carefully for a few days on the actual flow. He then decides to what extent any continued less-than-profitable decisions and actions by Glen are due to a real indifference to profit, and takes appropriate steps.

THE ESSENCE OF THIS APPROACH

Ike goes to the very heart of the problem before assuming that Glen is to blame.

ADAPTING THESE SOLUTIONS TO YOUR OWN WORK

Before you hire a new man in a position as important as dispatcher, make sure that you:

- Have foolproof procedures and forms for him to function with maximum/optimum company profit as his objective.
- Have explained them adequately to all concerned.

SITUATION NUMBER 29 — The new hire who feels superior to his boss.

INCIDENT

Irv Daley had been quality control supervisor in a large chemical company. That company merged with a conglomerate and Irv was shuffled out of a job.

Jack Eastmore was production manager of a medium-sized manufacturing company that had a vacancy for a quality control manager. Irv had a chemical engineering degree and was twenty-four years old. Jack, who graduated from high school twenty years ago, had gone no further in his formal education and had been with the company ever since he got his diploma. Jack knew just about everything he needed to know about his job.

An employment agency brought Irv and Jack's company together and, after following the established procedure, Jack agreed that Irv should be hired.

Shortly afterwards Jack noticed the following:

- Irv was sometimes surly about differences of opinion between them regarding product quality.
- Jack would hear rumors that Irv went about grumbling about having to take orders from a man who was less qualified than he in the matter of technical knowledge related to Irv's job.

ALTERNATE SOLUTIONS

A. As long as Irv does a completely acceptable job, Jack can ignore the grumbling and the rumors.

THE ESSENCE OF THIS APPROACH

Eventually Irv may stop grumbling and complaining. Jack has thus avoided an undesirable confrontation. If the grumbling does not stop, there will be time enough to do something about it later.

B. Jack can make it his business, from time to time, to drop in on Irv.

He seeks occasions for doing the following:

- Praising Irv's work where he deserves it.
- Subtly making suggestions for quality decisions which show a real superiority on his part to Irv's abilities.
- Telling Irv how fortunate he — Jack — is that he has, in this position, a man of Irv's excellent academic background which, when Irv has been around long enough, will make him a real contributor to the profitability of the company.

THE ESSENCE OF THIS APPROACH

Jack tries to accomplish two things simultaneously:

- He builds Irv's ego up.
- He wins Irv's respect.

ADAPTING THESE SOLUTIONS TO YOUR OWN WORK

A new hire may or may not have the same attitude toward you that you want him to have. It might be well to emphasize the proper attitude in the orientation you give him before he starts on his new assignment.

If he begins to show a failure to respect you, find out why and try to set him on the right track. If he persists in his lack of respect for you, try to ascertain the cause; then see whether the cause can be eliminated. If it can't, *he* may have to be.

SITUATION NUMBER 30 — The new hire who earned more money on his last job.

INCIDENT

Wade Zeamer had recently been hired to head up a new safety management job under Jerry Fairbanks. Wade's job was definitely outside of the wage and salary jurisdiction of both the state and federal laws. He was unquestionably part of management in the company. On a number of occasions Jerry asked Wade to finish up certain safety statistics before leaving the office at the end of the regular working time, since they were needed just as soon as the office opened the next day. Wade gave a number of excuses for not being able to stay beyond the regular time.

One day when Jerry decided to ask Wade whether there was anything bothering him, Wade said: "Well, I earned more money on my last job and never had to stay beyond the regular day to do my work."

ALTERNATE SOLUTIONS

A. Jerry can make some kind of noncommittal reply, drop the subject and start looking for Wade's replacement. As soon as he found one, he could tell Wade that his attitude was unacceptable to the company and that he was therefore being given notice.

THE ESSENCE OF THIS APPROACH

The probability is that Wade's attitude transcends his displeasure with the hours and the pay. He may just not be happy with his decision to have accepted this job. Jerry is better off getting rid of Wade before Wade quits.

B. Jerry can tell Wade:

- You knew, when you took the job, that we weren't budgeted for more than we offered you.
- I told you at that time that we'd give you more just as soon as your work showed you eligible for our normal increase program.
- Is there something other than the money bothering you? If so, let's talk about it.
- Either you're willing to feel and act like management at our company, despite your dissatisfaction with your pay, or you're really not interested in the job.
- If you decide that you want to merit being on our management team, please don't tell anyone about your attitude toward pay and do what you have to enthusiastically.
- Otherwise, tell me your real feeling and we'll arrange to give you notice and replace you.

THE ESSENCE OF THIS APPROACH

Jerry lays it on the line to Wade, but gives him the benefit of the doubt and another chance.

ADAPTING THESE SOLUTIONS TO YOUR OWN WORK

It's generally not wise to hire someone who has earned more at his previous job. He tends to be disgruntled from the start and may simply be hanging on while looking for a better job.

If, however, you have — for whatever good reason — decided to hire such an individual, impress on him from the very beginning that he must be completely content with his pay until he merits normal increases.

If he still shows that he's unhappy with his new job because of the pay, you have to decide whether it's even worthwhile to give him another chance. If you do, it should be clear to him that he risks his job if he doesn't really change his attitude.

6

How to Handle
The Employee
With Undesirable Productivity

In the following situations notice how the manager makes it clear to his assistants what is meant by productivity, what kinds of results make for desirable productivity and their absolute responsibility and accountability for it. Note, also, how he pinpoints various causes of undesirable productivity and helps to remove them.

SITUATION NUMBER 31 — Undesirable productivity due to an attitude against conscientiousness.

INCIDENT

Julie Gall had been hired as an assistant to the general manager, Manny Haines. His job called for him to undertake a considerable number of miscellaneous duties, some repetitive and some one-time. In all cases he exercised only such authority as was specifically given to him.

Manny took a great deal of care in looking for a candidate for the position and, when he interviewed Julie, made it quite plain to him not only what the job entailed but also that his main function was to relieve Manny of many details not meriting Manny's taking time away from his major tasks in order to accomplish them.

Julie had been very enthusiastic about the job and seemed at first to apply himself most assiduously to it. Lately, however, Manny has been finding that he has been getting less work out of Julie than the job called for, particularly in these specific ways:

- Julie took excessively long breaks with people whom he liked.
- He was frequently on the phone with his wife.
- He often left his office with no trace of his whereabouts.
- He spent more time on — and gave priority to — those tasks he liked, often deferring beyond deadlines those he didn't care for.

ALTERNATE SOLUTIONS

A. Manny can ask Julie to sit down with him and tell him:

- Here's what I've noticed in your results lately.
- What's the reason?
- Do you want to improve?

THE ESSENCE OF THIS APPROACH

Manny comes right to the point, gives Julie a chance to tell his side of the story and asks him what he wants to do about it.

B. Manny can ask Julie to sit down with him and do the following:

- Tell him that he — Manny — has observed a lessening of satisfactory productivity on Julie's part.
- Say that the trouble may lie with a failure of effective communication between them as to what the job calls for.
- Indicate that he therefore wants to review the job, and do so.
- Express confidence that Julie will do better now that there is no doubt about what he's supposed to do.

THE ESSENCE OF THIS APPROACH

Manny takes a positive attitude, giving Julie every chance to vindicate himself, regardless of what his attitude has been.

C. Manny can point out to Julie the areas in which he has fallen down. He can say that in all other respects Julie is doing an acceptable job, and then lay the law down in no uncertain terms that Julie is not to continue to indulge in those undesirable practices without the risk of losing his job.

THE ESSENCE OF THIS APPROACH

Manny focuses on the real areas of undesirable productivity right away. He also gives Julie the necessary praise to counterbalance the unpleasantness of the other statements.

ADAPTING THESE SOLUTIONS TO YOUR OWN WORK

An assistant whose results fall below expectations may just not understand or be aware of the concept of conscientiousness regarding productivity. In such a case, the emphasis should be on making him aware of how important it is to work hard and continuously if productivity is to be kept high. Wasting time is not always malicious, but the time-waster must learn to stop being one.

SITUATION NUMBER 32 — Undesirable productivity due to constant indulgence in personal matters.

INCIDENT

Max Haley is operations manager of a manufacturing company. His chief inspector is Phil Ince. Phil has seven inspectors under him, and his main job is to move among them all the time, making sure that they are doing their work properly. These inspectors are salaried employees.

Max has noticed an unusually large number of quality rejections and asked Phil about it. Phil attributed the excess to poor raw materials and negligence on the part of the production foremen. Max investigated and discovered that:

• Only a small part of the trouble lay in poor raw materials.

- Most of the foremen were doing a good job.
- Natural, minor faults develop in the components which could easily be corrected if discovered early enough.
- Phil's inspectors aren't catching these sufficiently.
- Phil is not touring the plant to supervise his inspectors with proper frequency.
- Phil spends a great deal of time in his office on personal phone calls and personal paperwork.
- Phil socializes excessively with other employees, either in his own office or theirs.

ALTERNATE SOLUTIONS

A. Max can simply tell Phil that he is spending too much time on personal matters, that this is adversely affecting his supervision, which is in turn resulting in poor quality, and that Max must desist from this unjustifiable practice.

THE ESSENCE OF THIS APPROACH

Max simply asserts his authority in a no-nonsense way, because the reason for the poor productivity is absolutely untenable.

B. Max can ask the controller to run a study on the costs to the company resulting from rejections. He then calls in both the purchasing agent and the production superintendent to meet with him and Phil. At this session he develops the following discussion:

- An acceptance of the unnecessary rejection cost.
- An effort to arrive at the real causes for the excessive rejections.
- A request that all concerned do better to cut down on rejections.

To the extent that that meeting has probably established that faulty inspection has materially contributed to heavy rejections, Max can then say to Phil:

- Poor inspection is your accountability.
- I know only one way to shore it up: your increased presence among your inspectors.
- Please spend more time with them.

THE ESSENCE OF THIS APPROACH

Max makes Phil realize the problem in a strictly objective way. He shows Phil the solution without reference to the unprofessional attention to personal matters, thus avoiding embarrassment.

C. Wholly aside from the impact that Phil's attention to personal matters is having on rejections, Max can tell Phil that:

- Max has evidence that Phil is spending more time on personal matters than a man of his position should, especially since this could serve as a bad example.
- Max wants Phil to put a stop to this practice.

THE ESSENCE OF THIS APPROACH

Max uses Phil's undesirable productivity due to excessive personal business as a springboard for tackling the basic problem of unwise management waste of time. This can carry over to any other bad result from that practice.

ADAPTING THESE SOLUTIONS TO YOUR OWN WORK

Whatever the reason for low productivity by a manager, he must be made firmly and promptly aware of the result and its seriousness. If the cause is an unprofessional use of company time for excessive personal business, the emphasis must be on *two* corrective actions: one to increase the productivity by eliminating the waste and the other to eliminate the undesirable practice wholly aside from its effect on productivity, as a matter of professionalism in management.

SITUATION NUMBER 33 — Undesirable productivity due to an inability to do the expected work.

INCIDENT

Roy Kahn had been foreman over one part of the yard. When a vacancy occurred for superintendent, his boss — the operations manager, Sam LaFarge — named Roy to the position, with the latter's consent.

Roy had been a very able foreman, but the overall yard productivity began to slip badly shortly after Roy took over.

Sam's investigation revealed that Roy, who was very competent in managing workers, was having difficulty managing foremen. He seemed to be afraid to give them orders because he had so recently been one of them.

ALTERNATE SOLUTIONS

A. Roy can be asked to meet with Sam and all of the foremen. Sam, without indicating what the problem is, can raise the following points for consideration:

- Foremen have to have a superintendent.
- That man has to give orders and the foremen must obey them.
- Sam has appointed Roy to that job because he has confidence in Roy.
- Will all the men help Roy to meet his obligations in his new job?

THE ESSENCE OF THIS APPROACH

Sam, without letting on any weakness of Roy, spells out the authority that Roy has, Sam's confidence in Roy and good reasons why the foremen should help him.

B. Sam can spend many hours with Roy on the job. Without bypassing Roy, he would thus be lending his own authority to Roy. Whenever Roy falters Sam can quietly buoy him up.

THE ESSENCE OF THIS APPROACH

Sam tries to fit Roy to the job before coming to a conclusion that he had picked the wrong man.

ADAPTING THESE SOLUTIONS TO YOUR OWN WORK

To begin with, before you elevate a man to a higher management position, make sure he has the stature and confidence. If you think he has the promise to exercise the right kind of authority, watch him very carefully during the first weeks. Move along with him from time to time.

If you detect a drop in productivity which seems to stem from his weak management of his foremen, take him aside and try to find out why. If it's a matter of fear of unpopularity from his former fellows, try to bolster him up and belittle the fear. Where advisable, appeal to the other foremen for cooperation, without indicating the weakness.

In the last analysis, if productivity still stays low or gets worse because of this same weakness, you may have to admit you erred in appointing him. Unfortunately, in such cases, you may have to separate him, since demotion generally doesn't work out.

SITUATION NUMBER 34 — Undesirable productivity due to a lack of knowledge of what's expected of him.

INCIDENT

Sid Maguire was in charge of a project involving the production of a given number of components per month at a cost not to exceed a stated figure. He had several different departments assigned to him for this purpose, each headed by a foreman. Tony Napal was Sid's boss.

The customer for whom the project had been started was complaining that he wasn't receiving the number of components promised and needed for each month. Investigation revealed that the fault didn't lie with the traffic department. Also, the controller's statements indicated that the cost of the company for producing what components *were* produced exceeded the estimate on which the price had been based, thus cutting down considerably on the expected profit.

Tony had a long conference with Sid and discovered that this poor productivity was due to Sid's really not knowing the pace at which production had to proceed if schedules were to be met, and allowing his foremen to explain away as only temporary setbacks their failure to yield the required production for the month.

As to the cost, Tony found out that much of it went into rework of expensive materials, which often resulted in the scrapping of many of them. This rework was also one of the causes of the bad productivity.

ALTERNATE SOLUTIONS

A. Tony could insist that Sid had to spend more time out in the production areas, paying very close attention to the following points:

- Which foremen were not doing their jobs of supervision and guidance as well as they should.
- Which workers didn't know exactly what they were supposed to do, and/or how to do it well.
- Whether there were any facilities lacking, in poor condition or not at hand.
- Whether raw materials were available when needed.
- Whether the number of workers was sufficient or, perhaps, excessive.
- Any other factors which were contributing to the poor productivity.

Sid was then to report to Tony on these items so that together they could remedy any situations calling for it.

THE ESSENCE OF THIS APPROACH

Tony throws the burden of making sure that all concerned know exactly what's expected of them on Sid. Sid is also required to ascertain any other factors which cause the trouble. When Sid reports this to Tony they can work the solutions out together.

B. Tony can spend more time out in the production areas himself, to find out why productivity is so poor and costs are so high. He can then point out to Sid not only what the problem is but perhaps the fact that Sid should have looked into these matters himself and either remedied them himself or pointed out to Tony where he needed Tony's remedial help.

THE ESSENCE OF THIS APPROACH

Tony can discover whether it is really Sid who doesn't know exactly what's expected of him. Should that prove to be the case it's more important to decide what to do about Sid's ignorance (or carelessness) first, before tackling the problem on the foreman level.

C. Tony can set up a schedule for the completion of the components on a daily basis, including maximum costs per day for such completion. He then goes over this schedule with Sid to make sure that Sid understands it completely. Tony then gives Sid a form to complete at the end of each working day and give to him.

That form, properly designed for ease of filling out, should show:

- The number of components satisfactorily completed that day.
- The total expenditures for that day as outlined by appropriate captions on the form.
- Sid's explanations for any departure from the standards of performance for that day, as outlined on the form.

In this way Tony can decide on a daily basis what has to be done in order to prevent a day's poor productivity from mushrooming into a month's irremediably poor productivity.

THE ESSENCE OF THIS APPROACH

Tony makes it perfectly clear that Sid is expected to yield specific results on a daily basis. If in any one day Tony agrees with Sid's judgment of the reasons for poor productivity he can decide what has to be done that day — if at all — to assure remedying the situation.

ADAPTING THESE SOLUTIONS TO YOUR OWN WORK

When you want a certain kind and level of productivity from your assistants you mustn't assume that it is enough just to tell them what has to be done. They must clearly understand and agree to *all* of these requirements:

- The minimum number of units which must be completed by a certain time, preferably by day or slightly less frequent time periods.
- The exact quality of each unit before it can be considered as having been completed.
- The specific elements of cost within their control, which mustn't be exceeded.

You must also receive from them the kind of timely report which makes it possible for you to know whether they really understand and are properly performing before the harm becomes too great.

SITUATION NUMBER 35 — Undesirable productivity due to (suspected) alcoholism.

INCIDENT

Vick Radford was the company's chief job estimator. He reported to Abe Padilla. Vick had been with the company for some fifteen years and had generally been a very effective employee in whatever job he held. Lately Abe noticed that the estimators were slacking off in both the quantity and the quality of their work.

Abe spent a little more time than usual in investigation and came up with the following facts:

- Vick was having trouble, of a nature which Abe couldn't precisely define, at home.
- Vick was coming in late recently, always with a different excuse.
- Vick was often absent from work, his wife having called in advance to say that he was ill, frequently on a Monday.
- Vick's face seemed unduly flushed most of the time.
- Every once in a while — sometimes early in the morning and often right after lunch — Abe thought he smelled alcohol on Vick's breath.
- Vick seldom left his office to move about among his estimators.

- Abe noticed that the estimators tended to seem to be talking among themselves rather more than their jobs seemed to require.

ALTERNATE SOLUTIONS

A. Abe can ask Vick to sit down with him for a discussion along these lines:

- Your estimators' productivity has deteriorated considerably in the last few weeks.

- Were you aware of this?

- Do you know why?

- What do you intend to do about this?

THE ESSENCE OF THIS APPROACH

Abe gives Vick a chance to rectify the situation regarding productivity without at all bringing up the question of the suspected alcoholism. In this way, either it turns out that there *is* no alcoholism or, if there is, that Vick can prevent it from interfering with his effective work.

B. Abe can ask Vick whether he's having any kind of unusual problems at home. If Vick says that he is, Abe urges him to discuss them with him with a view toward seeing what can be done to prevent those problems from having an adverse impact on Vick's work, which Abe then describes as less effective than it used to be.

On the other hand, if Vick says that he's *not* having any problems at home, Abe can then ask him why he's not performing as well as he used to. Abe then urges Vick to do everything necessary to bring his results up to their former level.

THE ESSENCE OF THIS APPROACH

Abe gives Vick every opportunity to bring up problems related to the suspected alcoholism, without in any way hinting at it. If Vick gives any indication of such a problem Abe can suggest to Vick that he try to solve the problem, since it's adversely affecting his work, and that as much as Abe values Vick, Abe cannot permit his situation to continue to affect the productivity in his department the way it has been.

C. Abe can ask the company's industrial relations manager to launch a subtle investigation to discover whether Vick is an alcoholic. This can be done by a careful check of records and discreet inquiries both at the company and in the community.

The industrial relations manager's confidential oral report, backed up by confidential documentation, can then serve as a basis for a program of suggesting to Vick what his problem is and urging him to get professional help guided by the industrial relations manager.

THE ESSENCE OF THIS APPROACH

Abe confidentially initiates a truly professional investigation of a possible cause of the low productivity. Armed with the findings he can then proceed wisely and safely.

ADAPTING THESE SOLUTIONS TO YOUR OWN WORK

Alcoholism is such a frequent problem in American business — and it's worse in many countries abroad — that a good manager is always alert to the symptoms which might reveal that that condition exists. He must always be studying persistent cases of absenteeism, tardiness, early quits and low productivity to see whether patterns seem to exist suggesting the possibility that alcoholism is the cause. He must also carefully observe any changes in employee appearance, manner, behavior and breath for further clues.

He should, however, be very careful not to accuse or even hint to an employee that he has the alcoholism problem. It's best to give the employee an opportunity to bring the subject up himself. Alternately, a competent industrial relations manager knows how to help his colleague approach the problem.

SITUATION NUMBER 36 — Undesirable productivity due to lack of sufficient training.

INCIDENT

Alan O'Connell had been a very capable, conscientious and loyal hourly employee in the shop. A vacancy in the foreman ranks suddenly occurred because of an unexpected death. Alan was asked whether he'd like to fill the opening, and he willingly assented.

Within one day of his predecessor's demise Alan had been introduced to his new men — in a different department from his former one — and to the rest of the company, as the new foreman. Alan took up his foremanship duties at once. His boss was Toby Zak.

During the first month of Alan's foremanship productivity in his department dropped noticeably from what it had been under the recently deceased man. Toby made a deep study of the situation and of the causes of the problem and discovered that:

- Alan was working very hard.
- He did a lot of the work himself.
- He had no difficulty with the technical aspects of the processing.
- He spent a great deal of time in his office doing very necessary paperwork.
- At least half of his men were working at less than their usual productivity, and the quality of their finished components had deteriorated considerably.

ALTERNATE SOLUTIONS

A. Toby could ask Alan to read selected books on foremanship and/or send him to outside courses on the same subject, explaining that Alan needed this in order to add to his other excellent qualities and qualifications those dealing with foremanship itself, since, unfortunately, when the need arose for Alan's appointment as foreman there hadn't been time to give him the very necessary training in the art of foremanship.

THE ESSENCE OF THIS APPROACH

Toby removes from Alan all inferences of criticism, points out why he needs the training and arranges for it at times which do not cut into Alan's actual presence on the job.

B. Toby can arrange to spend several hours with Alan after work once or twice a week, and give him the necessary foremanship concepts. Toby then spends more time with Alan on the job than with the more experienced foremen, applying those concepts in Alan's daily rounds.

THE ESSENCE OF THIS APPROACH

Toby still doesn't take Alan away from his work and yet gives him a training program which is tailored to that company's and Toby's specific foremanship problems and needs.

C. Since Toby's other foremen may never have gotten the kind of training Alan needs, having overcome that weakness through costly experience, Toby can plan, devise and administer what he can call a refresher course in the art of foremanship for all of his assistants.

He announces the program to them in a way that none of them interprets the course as criticism and sets up a schedule of weekly meetings after hours, devoted exclusively to a "refresher" course in foremanship, blending concepts with specifics from their daily work, doctored so that no one recognized his own shortcomings in the examples (although he is directed to look into himself to see how applicable those specifics are to him). Alan would, of course, be part of this program.

THE ESSENCE OF THIS APPROACH

Toby trains Alan in an atmosphere of naturalness and great practicality at the same time that he gives his other men what they probably also need — a refresher (or perhaps brand new) course in the art of foremanship, which is bound to increase their own productivity.

ADAPTING THESE SOLUTIONS TO YOUR OWN WORK

When a vacancy occurs for a foreman, remember that the appointee must not only be knowledgeable and competent in the technology involved but must also be well versed in foremanship, which is an art in itself. Failure to do this is bound to result in lessened productivity.

To avoid having this problem you should either always have one good worker in after-hours foremanship training — with no promises of promotion — or train the new appointee in foremanship before you put him into the job; or get someone to become the foreman who has already had foremanship experience, whether outside or inside your company.

7

How to Handle
The Manager
Who Violates Company Policy

In the following situations notice that every company must have a certain number of fixed policies. These can be changed from time to time, but they must be communicated and enforced in the same way as the following situations exemplify the need for such communication and enforcement for existing policies.

SITUATION NUMBER 37 — The manager who violates company policy regarding notification of his whereabouts.

INCIDENT

Alvin Quinn is the supervisor of the purchasing section in charge of all requisitions not related to raw materials. He must, of necessity, move about a great deal.

The trouble is that many of the other managers of the company have to consult Alvin before they can effectively fill out certain of their requisitions. When this is necessary they often can't locate him in his office. Even his secretary doesn't always know where he is.

This results in frequent delays in the ability of those managers to complete their requests for needed tangibles and services that have to be bought on the outside, some as a result of suddenly appearing needs. They have complained about this to their and Alvin's boss, Stan Yanovich.

Company policy requires all managers to leave word of their whereabouts.

ALTERNATE SOLUTIONS

A. Stan can sit down with Alvin and tell him the following:

- Company policy requires every manager to leave word with a reliable assistant of where he — the manager — can always be reached during the business day.
- The reason for the policy is that other managers have frequent need to consult a manager who may be absent from his desk, in cases where their inability to reach him promptly can result in loss to the company of valuable time or other needs.
- Alvin's job does, of course, require him to be away from his desk with great frequency, and *his* position is more often critical for ready communicability than that of others.
- Therefore, Alvin simply must keep his secretary informed of where he is at all times, no matter how burdensome this might be.

THE ESSENCE OF THIS APPROACH

Stan makes Alvin aware of the policy, its importance to the company and Alvin's key position regarding that policy. He does so without criticism. Furthermore, in case his reasonable attitude doesn't work, he makes it plain to Alvin that he has no choice in the matter.

B. Stan can tell Alvin that he is hurting the company in two respects:

- He is violating company policy in not keeping his secretary consistently informed of his whereabouts. This hurts the company because every policy must be followed by everyone — consistently — or the company will function less efficiently.

- •This particular violation has the specific undesirable result of causing other managers to waste *their* time.

THE ESSENCE OF THIS APPROACH

Stan places the major emphasis on the violation, regardless of what it was. In this way he can not only make more likely Alvin's pursuit of the specific policy in question but also, perhaps, Alvin's increased awareness of the importance of following all established company policy.

ADAPTING THESE SOLUTIONS TO YOUR OWN WORK

Every management employee and many non-management employees must be able to be found when needed. This has to be made a company policy, effectively communicated and consistently enforced.

You must be constantly alert to situations where one manager or another violates this policy and when you discover one who does, you must re-emphasize the policy (and his obligation to follow all policies) and do whatever is necessary to get him to follow that particular policy.

SITUATION NUMBER 38 — The manager who violates company policy regarding duration of lunch time.

INCIDENT

Amos Sacks is in charge of ten office employees. He reports to Seymour Talley. Amos is competent and, when he is present among his assistants, conscientious. He is, however, a very friendly and sociable person. He's been around for a long time and has developed a number of cronies who are not all as devoted to work as he is.

Company policy is that there are two lunch periods: one from 12 to 12:30 and the other from 1 to 1:30. The unused half hour is needed for cleaning up the lunchroom between lunch periods. Policy says that managers as well as non-managers may use their lunchtime in any one of the following ways:

- Go to the lunchroom for lunch, either their own (brought from home) or that which is provided by the caterers.
- Go out of the building during their half hour.
- Stay at their desks reading or idling, but in dignified, businesslike fashion; however, no eating is allowed at the desks.

The policy goes on to say that the half hour must not begin before the stated time nor end after it.

Amos frequently leaves before his half hour and/or returns after his half hour.

ALTERNATE SOLUTIONS

A. Seymour can talk to Amos as follows:

- Company policy requires that no manager be away for lunch beyond the allotted half hour (unless previous permission is granted).
- Amos frequently violates this policy.
- Why?

Seymour can then tackle the cause and try to eliminate it.

THE ESSENCE OF THIS APPROACH

Seymour reminds Amos of a company policy and points out Amos' violation thereof without criticism. He tries to get Amos to "reform" or explain that he is justified.

B. Seymour can simply tell Alvin that:

- He has lately been taking more time away from his desk — presumably for lunch — than company policy permits.
- The policy provides for seeking and, where appropriate, getting permission to extend the lunch period for valid reasons, in which case alternative managerial coverage has to be provided.
- Regardless of the reasons for past policy violation, it is to cease.

THE ESSENCE OF THIS APPROACH

Alvin places emphasis on the importance of obeying the policy, at the same time that he repeats the safeguard that Alvin has in asking for extensions where necessary.

C. Seymour can personally supervise Alvin's area whenever he is violating that particular policy and document the undesirable results of his unauthorized lunch-period extensions. He then sits down with Alvin and:

- Reminds him of the policy.
- Repeats the reasons for the policy.
- Reveals his documentation as validation of the wisdom of the policy.
- Asks Alvin to conform to the policy not only because of the attendant problems but also for the sake of obeying policy.

THE ESSENCE OF THIS APPROACH

Seymour appeals to Alvin's sense of obligation and reason, proves the validity of the policy and then requests compliance for the two reasons: obeying policy per se and the harm that derives from not obeying it.

ADAPTING THESE SOLUTIONS TO YOUR OWN WORK

Every minute of the working day costs the company money, regardless of whether any one or more of its employees are currently being as productive as they should be. Company policy must therefore carefully provide for the proper proportion of productivity from the standpoint of actual time put in by employees.

One of the most common time wastes is that of employees who leave early for lunch or come back late. Adequate provision must, of course, be made for exceptional cases when more time for lunch is justified.

Policy must be firmly established and enforced. Offenders can be set back on the track in a number of ways, depending on your management philosophy and/or the circumstances peculiar to your company. The policy must be enforced uniformly, however, not only because of the loss to the company from its being flouted but also because a policy is a policy — to be either enforced or repealed and modified.

SITUATION NUMBER 39 — The manager who violates company policy regarding the favoring of one employee over another.

INCIDENT

Arnie Zelden was promoted to be the new office manager. He had a large number of people in his department and therefore a number of supervisors who now reported to him as they had to his predecessor. Arnie had himself been a supervisor until his advancement.

Arnie had the opportunity to reorganize his department, because his boss Ray Baff thought he should be given a free hand to prove his ability to fill his new position effectively.

Arnie decided to divide his department into three major sections, each with an appropriate head and each having a number of supervisors under him. This would, justifiably, reduce Arnie's span of control to a more manageable degree.

Arnie selected as one of the recommended section heads one of his previous fellow supervisors, Rube Abbruzzi. Rube had been a competent supervisor, but there was some question about his ability to handle other supervisors. Arnie favored Rube because they were good friends both outside and inside the company. Ray, however, felt that another supervisor, Percy Caine, was better qualified than Rube for one of the positions as section head.

The company's policy regarding not putting favoritism above merit was clearly established and known to all.

ALTERNATE SOLUTIONS

A. Ray can tell Arnie that he cannot go along with his recommendation of Rube, and that he wants Percy to get the post, explaining his judgment that Percy is superior to Rube and that Arnie is to work with Percy as though he had been his own choice.

•

THE ESSENCE OF THIS APPROACH

Ray overlooks the violation of the company policy because:

- He's going to overcome the effect of this particular act of favoritism.
- He's going to force Percy on Arnie and doesn't want to beat the latter down too much.
- Arnie will probably get the message anyway.

B. Ray can ask Arnie to make a careful analysis of the qualifications of both men and sit down with him to discuss them. Ray then sees to it that Arnie gets to realize and admit that Percy is the better man, and that he is therefore changing his mind and recommending Percy.

THE ESSENCE OF THIS APPROACH

Ray causes Arnie to use good managerial analysis and judgment, voluntarily changing his previous position and therefore in effect admitting that he had violated the rule against favoritism.

C. Ray can bluntly point out to Arnie that he has played favorites, contrary to company policy, and that he is going to have to accept Ray's decision because he — Arnie — had lost his option because of his violation.

THE ESSENCE OF THIS APPROACH

Ray teaches Arnie a lesson about company policy which may lead to a conscious avoidance by him of similar violations.

ADAPTING THESE SOLUTIONS TO YOUR OWN WORK

It's always a good idea to discuss appointments to be made by an assistant directly with that assistant. In this way, any tenddency he may have to violate policy — as for example in playing favorites — can be nipped in the bud with minimal lowering of morale or losing of face.

SITUATION NUMBER 40 — The manager who violates company policy regarding the authorization of overtime work.

INCIDENT

Archie Cannon is chief draftsman in Murray Wooster's engineering department. Murray has told Archie that it is company policy that, except in an emergency where Murray is unavailable, Archie is never to authorize overtime work for his draftsmen without Murray's approval.

Archie has had some of his men work overtime without such approval on several occasions. It seems that most of these times were when Murray was out of the office for the afternoon on company business.

Murray has reminded Archie each time that he — Murray — thought the overtime was unjustified according to the company policy. Each time Archie claimed to have a good excuse.

Murray wants to cut down on the amount of overtime Archie is using.

ALTERNATE SOLUTIONS

A. Murray can make a careful work-load study of Archie's draftsmen during the regular working day and try to find out why so much overtime is necessary. Included in this study would have to be an assessment of the quantity and quality of their productivity and of Archie's supervision.

THE ESSENCE OF THIS APPROACH

Murray goes to the core of the problem with a view toward trying to eliminate the cause of the overtime. This does not, of course, overcome the problem of possible violation in itself, regardless of what the violation happens to be.

B. Murray can spell out the rules even more carefully, perhaps providing a number where he can be reached whenever

Archie thinks that an emergency exists and Murray is out at the time.

THE ESSENCE OF THIS APPROACH

Murray cuts down on the possibility of either a violation or of an excuse for it which sounds plausible, at least to Archie.

C. Murray can sit down with Archie and talk to him along these lines:

- The overtime has been excessive.
- Much of it wasn't really necessary.
- You may have been sincere in your belief that the over-time was necessary and that you should authorize it be-cause I was unavailable.
- I'm going to continue the same policy as before, but unless your judgment regarding this overtime situation improves, I'm going to have to conclude that you are lacking in this very important managerial skill/attitude, and I'll have to take the authority for approving overtime away from you completely.

THE ESSENCE OF THIS APPROACH

Murray meets the basic issue of failing to adhere to company policy — for whatever reason — and tells Archie that he has only one more chance to prove that he deserves the applicable managerial authority.

ADAPTING THESE SOLUTIONS TO YOUR OWN WORK

Overtime is a very costly practice. Not only do you pay more for it than you do for straight time, but you also run into these problems:

- Less than conscientious employees will, consciously or otherwise, try to assure overtime if they know they can get it.
- They often tire themselves more during straight time,

trying to assure such overtime, than they would if no overtime were possible.

- Productivity is generally lower during the overtime hours.

The rule, therefore, should be that there is absolutely no overtime without the decision of a management employee who:

- Values the importance of the no-overtime rule.
- Will do everything profitably possible to avoid overtime.
- Will exercise his overtime-authorization authority with proper managerial judgment.

And, above all, whenever one of your assistants does violate your rule regarding overtime, remember that there are two issues involved:

1. Why did he violate the policy, regardless of the cause for the overtime?
2. Why was the overtime necessary?

SITUATION NUMBER 41 — The manager who violates company policy regarding employee evaluations.

INCIDENT

Anne Dallek works for Estelle Waites. Company policy requires every supervisor to evaluate employees twice a year at stated times. The policy includes a provision that the evaluator must be thoroughly objective, playing no favorites and practicing no unfairness.

After the latest evaluation one of the clerks comes to see Anne to ask why her evaluation was unsatisfactory when she felt that she had consistently performed as well as another clerk — marked superior — in the same section. When Ann stuck to her guns that the evaluations were accurate, the complaining clerk asked Anne to accompany her to see Estelle.

Estelle listened to both sides of the story and told both of them that she'd make a decision later and let them know.

Estelle's investigation revealed that Anne had indeed played favorites by marking superior an employee who always played up to her but whose work was no better than satisfactory. She also concluded that the unsatisfactory rating of the complainant was justified.

ALTERNATE SOLUTIONS

A. Estelle can insist that Anne revise the superior rating to read simply satisfactory, with an apology to the employee whom she had improperly overrated. Estelle can then call both Anne and the complainant in and explain:

- That the superior rating had been an oversight.
- That the complainant's work wasn't even up to the mere satisfactory rating of the other employee.
- That the complainant could qualify for even the highest rating if she applied herself, and that Anne was ready to help her at all times.

THE ESSENCE OF THIS APPROACH

Estelle saves Anne's face as best she can but still has the correct ratings prevail and potentially accepted by all concerned.

B. Estelle can call both Anne and the complainant in and tell the complainant the following:

- Ratings are always applied as objectively and as fairly as possible.
- The employee rated doesn't always see the causes for the rating, despite all efforts to explain them.
- Her rating was absolutely accurate and she has every opportunity to do better next time.
- Estelle can't permit one employee to complain about another's rating; this is strictly a management matter.

Estelle then reads the riot act to Anne, emphasizing the embarrassment that Anne caused Estelle and cautioning her not to depart again from this or any other company policy.

THE ESSENCE OF THIS APPROACH

Estelle completely saves Anne's face, insists that the complainant's rating was accurate — which it was — and then takes steps to prevent Anne from violating that and other company policies.

ADAPTING THESE SOLUTIONS TO YOUR OWN WORK

Employee evaluation is a very difficult management activity to administer and enforce properly. Actually, the most profitable method is one which combines all of the following elements:

- Every management employee must constantly be evaluating every one of his assistants.
- All significant observations must be carefully documented.
- Just as soon as possible after a management employee observes anything unusual — good or bad — in an assistant, the latter's attention must be appropriately drawn to it, and praise or criticism promptly applied (as appropriate) — the latter to be followed by corrective measures.
- The employee must continually be kept informed of his progress and of his satisfactory, unsatisfactory or outstanding performance — on a weekly or monthly basis, with specifics where appropriate.

If the company then wants to have a formal evaluation system, it's more efficient and effective. Whether the evaluation is formal or informal, the following standards must be communicated and enforced:

- Continuing observation.
- Careful and accurate judgments.
- Objective and correct evaluations.

Your policies and procedures on *your* evaluation system must be effectively communicated and strictly enforced. Violators must be studied in order to ascertain the causes of the deviations: inability and/or improper attitudes. Not only must the results of poor evaluations be in themselves properly corrected, but the violators must be apprised of the fact of the violation and the absolute need for avoiding repeated violations — for both the avoidance of undesired results and the mere fact of violation.

8

How to Handle The Undesirable Management of Records and Reports

In the following situations notice how frequent such mismanagement is, and the reasons for it. Many management employees as well as many non-management employees don't like to keep records and write reports — or if they do, they may not have the kind of high standards you want for such records and reports. You should, of course, keep paperwork down to the barest minimum consistent with profitability, but what you must have must be properly enforced. Make sure that your assistants know your standards for such paperwork and how to do it well; then see to it that it doesn't interfere with their other duties — and vice versa. Finally, catch the mismanagement before it goes too far and correct it.

SITUATION NUMBER 42 — The manager who always sends reports in late.

INCIDENT

Art Eaton is a production foreman. Mort Unterman is his superintendent. Mort has explained very carefully, to all of his foremen, that the daily report on number of units completed per man must be on his desk by the beginning of the shift the following work day. Art's reports generally do not get to Mort's desk until about the middle of the day.

ALTERNATE SOLUTIONS

A. Mort can spend a few days in Art's work area in order to see why Art's reports come in late. If he discovers that Art is really tied up with legitimate activities which prevent his sending the reports in on time, he can take the appropriate corrective measures. On the other hand, if he discovers that Art is simply inefficient or indifferent to the report duty, he can take those appropriate steps.

THE ESSENCE OF THIS APPROACH

Mort finds out at once why Art isn't sending the reports in on time. This makes for greater effectiveness and efficiency in handling the problem, whatever it is.

B. Mort can call Art in and talk to him in this manner:

- The daily production report is extremely important.
- I must have it on my desk the first thing in the morning in order to correct any bad scheduling or production before it becomes too costly.
- You simply must have that report on my desk on time.

THE ESSENCE OF THIS APPROACH

Mort makes clear to Art how important the report is and places the burden of compliance squarely where it belongs.

C. Mort can talk to Art as follows:

- You're the only foreman whose daily production report reaches me late on a continual basis.
- I want you to prepare and give me by the first day of next week a brief, written explanation of why you are the only one whose reports are late.

THE ESSENCE OF THIS APPROACH

Mort puts the burden on Art to justify his delays or have to admit that there is no valid reason for them. Mort can then act accordingly.

ADAPTING THESE SOLUTIONS TO YOUR OWN WORK

If you require a report from an assistant, make sure that the deadline you establish for the receipt of that report is both important and reasonable; then insist that that deadline must be kept. Where it isn't, find out why.

If any of your assistants can make out a plausible justification for his delay, either remedy the cause of the delay or readjust the deadline. In any case, however, once you've decided that the deadline is achievable and proper, insist that it be met.

SITUATION NUMBER 43 — The employee whose handwriting is difficult to read.

INCIDENT

Bert Fales is a telephone order clerk, working under the supervision of Doug Gale. Doug, in turn, reports to Floyd Hall.

Floyd has been receiving complaints from various department heads who have to process all telephone orders that Bert's handwriting is frequently difficult to read, causing either unprofitable delays or actual errors.

Floyd has asked Doug about Bert's work and has consistently received the evaluation that Bert is very capable, conscientious and quick.

ALTERNATE SOLUTIONS

A. Floyd can ask Doug to sit down with Bert and point out the following to him:

- Bert's work is greatly appreciated.
- His desire for speed is well understood.
- Speed must not be permitted to cause delays or errors.

- Bert must make a great effort to have all of his order-writing legible.

THE ESSENCE OF THIS APPROACH

Going through the proper channels, Floyd makes Bert aware of his undesirable practice against a background of praise for his positive merit and impresses him with the importance of making the necessary efforts toward legibility.

B. Floyd can sit down with Doug and speak to him as follows:

- Were you aware that Bert's handwriting was difficult to read?
- If not, why not; if yes, why didn't you take the necessary effective measures?
- Either tell me that Bert's handwriting is irremediably illegible (in which case we'll give him a different assignment) or remedy the situation and report back to me when this has been accomplished.

THE ESSENCE OF THIS APPROACH

Floyd first explores the quality of Doug's management regarding Bert's shortcoming. Then Floyd addresses himself to the immediate problem and sets Doug the task of solving it.

ADAPTING THESE SOLUTIONS TO YOUR OWN WORK

Legibility in an employee's writing where that writing goes to other employees as an important part of necessary paper flow, is absolutely essential, for reasons of profitability as well as for reasons of morale. If a particular employee is assigned to write anything, his writing *must* be legible.

If his writing is irremediably illegible but he is otherwise profitably productive, he must be transferred to another job not involving his writing legibly.

In any event, the legibility of employee writing is the responsibility of that employee's immediate superior. Continuing employee illegibility, without appropriate action, is a *management* fault.

SITUATION NUMBER 44 — The foreman who is not sufficiently literate.

INCIDENT

George Indie has been a foreman with the company for twenty years, having been an hourly employee for ten years previously. George never went beyond sixth grade and has difficulty in reading and writing, but is a crackerjack foreman, whose men's productivity is consistently high. The only trouble is that George's reports are badly written and inaccurate. George also has difficulty reading written orders and directives.

Harry Jacmore has just been made superintendent, and George has become one of his new assistants. Harry has already become aware of George's literacy problem and feels that it is affecting Harry's ability to keep his department's paperwork up to snuff.

ALTERNATE SOLUTIONS

A. Harry can ask his boss to approve George's transfer to a different company function not involving paperwork, replacing George with another foreman more competent in that area.

THE ESSENCE OF THIS APPROACH

George is moved to another department where he can be useful and unhampered by his illiteracy. Meanwhile, Harry can run his department better because he not only puts a good foreman in place of George but also makes possible higher standards of departmental paperwork.

B. Harry can arrange for George to be tutored in the necessary subjects, thus upgrading his ability to cope with the necessary paperwork.

THE ESSENCE OF THIS APPROACH

Harry retains a competent foreman and attacks the problem of his one weakness.

C. Harry can assign to George an assistant to the foreman, whose responsibilities revolve exclusively around the administrative aspects of George's work. The assistant would have no authority over any of George's men, acting strictly in a nonline capacity with regard to them.

THE ESSENCE OF THIS APPROACH

George is permitted to continue to make his most valuable contribution to profit, while his weakness is shored up by an employee whose only responsibility is the adminsitration of records and the completion of reports.

ADAPTING THESE SOLUTIONS TO YOUR OWN WORK

To the extent that it is possible, don't appoint anyone to a position calling for paperwork who lacks the ability to do it. If he's good management material, put him into a condition of learning what he can't do before appointing him.

If, however, you inherit an assistant whose educational achievement falls short of your standards for him, either:

- Upgrade him where he is lacking, or
- If his contribution justifies it, hire someone to do what *he* cannot do, or
- Move him to a different position and replace him with someone who has *all* of the qualities needed for the job.

SITUATION NUMBER 45 — The supervisor who leaves important data out.

INCIDENT

Herb Unger is a foreman in charge of the fabrication of parts which must be assembled for components. His boss, Moe Kaiser, has been trying to analyze the profitability of the production in Herb's section, but finds a major problem in this: Moe cannot accurately allocate the number of acceptable parts from Herb's men, which result from rework due to unacceptable quality.

The production reports which Herb must turn in to Moe provide for the filling in of such information, but the relevant portion of those reports is either left blank from time to time or filled in in such a way that it isn't clear whether all of the required data are there.

ALTERNATE SOLUTIONS

A. Moe can call Herb in and show him the last few reports for his section. Moe can point out to Herb the gaps and discrepancies and ask Herb why he has left the important data out.

If Herb doesn't have a good excuse, Moe would then tell Herb that:

- Every portion of the form must be filled out properly.
- The omitted or incomplete data are important for stated reasons.
- Herb's overall performance as a foreman will be judged on the basis of *all* of his work.
- Repeated failure to complete the form properly could result in the need for Moe to consider very seriously whether Herb was suited for his important responsibility.

THE ESSENCE OF THIS APPROACH

Moe gives Herb a chance to explain his neglect, with proper caution on the consequences of his failure to improve.

B.   Moe can sit down with Herb and talk to him along these lines:

- Your work is generally satisfactory.
- You have the potential to be an outstanding and well rewarded management employee of the company.
- Your reports leave something to be desired; this could stand in the way of your realizing that potential.
- The area of your neglect is very serious because the data you leave out are essential for me to know the real results you are achieving, as well as to make certain important production decisions affecting the whole company.

Moe then shows Herb exactly where he is deficient and points out how easy it is for Herb to remedy the weakness. Moe closes the interview with an expression of confidence that Herb can and will overcome the shortcoming.

THE ESSENCE OF THIS APPROACH

Moe encourages Herb at the same time that he makes him aware of a potential impediment to his progress. Moe also goes into detail on the reasons for the emphasis on the data in question, thus providing additional motivation to Herb.

ADAPTING THESE SOLUTIONS TO YOUR OWN WORK

You must carefully read every report you receive from your assistants as promptly as possible. The time to call to their attention any data they omit is just as soon as you discover it.

You should then immediately point out the weakness, try to find out why it takes place, offer constructive help to solve the problem, and convince the assistant that he simply must not leave out any data called for, at the risk of creating the impression that he is making himself the judge of what you have a right to expect of him.

SITUATION NUMBER 46 — The timekeeper who doesn't know who's punching in for whom.

INCIDENT

Hy Jacobs is the plant timekeeper. Jed Lahey, his boss, happened to notice on a number of occasions that some of the men were punching in for others and made note of the names of the wrongdoers.

Hy has been presenting all of the time cards to Jed approved as punched. On no occasion has Hy called to Jed's attention any cases of one man punching in for another.

ALTERNATE SOLUTIONS

A. Jed can tell Hy what he has discovered and ask Hy why *he* hasn't been aware of the wrongdoing. Jed can then warn Hy that his job as timekeeper places very great emphasis on the ac-

curacy of the cards, which means that either he sees to it that no
one punches in for anyone else or he makes the appropriate nota-
tions in cases where someone violates the rule.

THE ESSENCE OF THIS APPROACH

Jed comes right to the point, re-emphasizes the importance
of accuracy of the cards and cautions Hy about the serious consequences of his continued failure to keep them accurate.

B. Jed can ask Hy what schedule he follows for supervising the punching-in process. If Hy says that he supervises
it very carefully, Jed can then ask him how come he hasn't
noticed what he — Jed — has. If Hy's response indicates anything less than a satisfactory schedule, Jed can point out to Hy
those specific examples of the undesirable results of such a
poor schedule and urge him to remedy the situation.

THE ESSENCE OF THIS APPROACH

Jed places the emphasis on Hy's supervisory activities which,
more than anything else, can determine his success in this situation, as in all others.

C. Jed can ask Hy to station himself at the place where the
time clock is situated — at least for as long as the problem exists
— and personally observe every man who punches in. Once the
wrong practice ceases, Hy can be asked to repeat such observation on an irregular basis.

THE ESSENCE OF THIS APPROACH

The men who are wrongly punching others in can be stopped
from doing it because of direct observation and necessary action.

ADAPTING THESE SOLUTIONS TO YOUR OWN WORK

Under no circumstances must employees be allowed to
punch in for others. A few men will ask others to do this for
them and some of these others will consent to do it.

The best way to prevent this is adequate supervision by a
responsible, conscientious and loyal management employee. If

he is there where the men punch in frequently, they will probably not risk it. If the practice does exist, the supervisor must increase the frequency of his presence where the punching in takes place.

SITUATION NUMBER 47 — The superintendent who pads the production figures.

INCIDENT

Les MacIntyre is one of the production superintendents under Milt Tamm. Milt requires a weekly report from all of his superintendents on actual production for the week. He discusses these reports at his monthly meetings and draws comparisons and contrasts among them.

Milt has noticed what appear to be discrepancies between Les' latest reports and the sales figures, coupled with inventory figures. His investigation reveals that Les always seems to be balanced in production figures for the quarter, but is short of quota some weeks (although his reports don't show this) and exceeds quota other weeks (also not shown). Milt concludes that Les can't meet quota consistently but does manage to straighten the situation out in the long run, covering up his peaks and valleys by doctoring the reports.

ALTERNATE SOLUTIONS

A. Milt can make a careful study of all of the facts, either retrospectively or prospectively.

If his investigation reveals beyond a doubt that Les is knowingly falsifying the figures, Milt should call Les in, confront him with the situation and give him a chance to prove that Milt was wrong in his conclusions.

If Milt cannot be convinced that there was an honest mistake, he has no choice but to dismiss Les for dishonesty.

THE ESSENCE OF THIS APPROACH

Milt makes a thorough investigation, gives Les a last chance and, if that chance reveals no change in the situation, does the only thing he can do if he is to maintain reliable assistants.

B. If investigation reveals that Les has actually been padding the figures, but Milt still needs and wants Les to continue to work for him, Milt can call Les in and tell him:

- What Milt has discovered.
- That Les has otherwise been doing a very valuable job.
- That Milt is gravely disappointed in Les.
- That Milt is willing to give Les another chance.
- That there is really no need to fear the truth about production.
- That Milt is ready to help Les solve any production problems he may have.
- That if there is a single case of dishonesty in the future, Les will immediately be dismissed.

THE ESSENCE OF THIS APPROACH

Milt can retain an otherwise valuable assistant without losing his own authoritativeness, while making it clear that there is to be no repetition of the padding or any other dishonesty.

ADAPTING THESE SOLUTIONS TO YOUR OWN WORK

The very first time that you sense that an assistant of yours is padding figures or otherwise misreporting, call him in. Ask him whether your inference is correct, giving him every opportunity to plead an honest error.

No matter how you handle the situation, however, never let anyone under you deceive you consciously about anything. Errors can be tolerated and corrected; poor judgment may be corrected too, in most cases, but dishonesty by an assistant on one occasion (perhaps excused that once, with a warning against repetition) usually leads to further dishonesty, a situation which you must not tolerate.

9

How to Handle Lack of Initiative and Drive

In the following situations notice that the first step is to make sure that this deficiency exists. An assessment must then be made of why the shortcoming is there and whether it is remediable. If it is, proper efforts must be made to make the manager aware of his weakness, to motivate him to shore it up with the appropriate strengths, to give him confidence that he can do so and to guide him to acquire the qualities involved.

SITUATION NUMBER 48 — The lack of initiative and drive regarding the discovery of improved techniques or methods.

INCIDENT

Lew Mackey was hired recently as production superintendent, having worked for years for a company in a similar business.

After Lew had gotten his feet sufficiently wet in the few ways in which his position differed from the one he had left, he came to one conclusion, among others: the materials handling in Mark Nash's production bay was at least for ten years behind the times.

Lew knew exactly what newer equipment was more efficient for that bay, and had cleared with his new boss that the

126

necessary budget for the required purchase was — and had long been — available.

Lew had two needs: to get the new equipment in as soon as profitably possible and to find out what, if anything, was wrong with Mark in view of his not having taken the initiative to ask for the new equipment between the time it had first become available and the time that Lew joined the company.

ALTERNATE SOLUTIONS

A. Lew can look into the records of his predecessor to see whether the latter was to blame rather than Mark. He can then take the appropriate action.

THE ESSENCE OF THIS APPROACH

Lew first rules out any plausible justification for Mark's not already having the new equipment.

B. Lew can sit down with Mark and hold this kind of conversation:

- As you know, I'm new here and am eager to benefit from the wisdom and experience of people like you.
- I've made a study of the materials-handling flow in all of my bays and have made note of the various bays where I will be wanting to ask questions of the various foremen.
- I'd like to know why this particular materials-handling setup (described) in your bay is still being used. Do you find it the best for your needs?

Depending on Mark's responses, Lew can:

- Come to a conclusion about Mark's knowledge of relevant equipment.
- Judge the state of Lew's initiative and drive.
- Take appropriate steps.

THE ESSENCE OF THIS APPROACH

Lew disarms Mark and gives him every opportunity to demonstrate that he is on top of things and possessed of the proper initiative and drive. Should this prove not to be so, Lew can then do what he has to both to correct the equipment situation and to upgrade Mark if possible.

C. Lew can ask Mark why he is still using the equipment in question. Mark's response would then guide Lew in how best to meet both problems: the equipment and Mark's foremanship.

THE ESSENCE OF THIS APPROACH

Lew goes right to the point that has sparked his asking Mark about the matter in question. Mark is immediately put on notice that something might be wrong and is given a chance to justify himself or reveal that there is no excuse for his passivity.

ADAPTING THESE SOLUTIONS TO YOUR OWN WORK

The responsibility for seeing to it that improved techniques and methods are always used (where not otherwise unprofitable) belongs to both the manager and his assistant. Where, however, the assistant is in a better position to know what's available and the need for it, his failure to act on it properly is a sign of weakness in initiative and drive. Not only must the manager address himself to the replacement of less effective and efficient equipment, etc.; he must also grapple with whether the assistant has or can have the proper drive.

SITUATION NUMBER 49 — The lack of initiative and drive regarding long-range planning.

INCIDENT

Marv O'Connor was a production foreman. His boss was Mike Paige. Marv was in the habit of requesting the recruitment of new workers only when he already needed them. Mike had urged Marv to change this habit and anticipate his needs, at least to alert the personnel people to be on the lookout.

One day Mike told all of his production foremen, including Marv, that within one month the workload would increase by a stated percentage for a period of at least one year. Mike urged them to start their planning at once and initiate within a few days the requisitioning procedure in preparation for the additional men they'd need.

One week before the new schedule was to go into effect Marv hadn't sent in any requisition for additional men.

ALTERNATE SOLUTIONS

A. Mike can give Marv a direct order to put in the necessary requisition, sending him a copy within a day. He would also tell Marv that he was disappointed in his record for initiative and use the current situation as a lesson for Marv's promise to do the required long-range planning in the future, with the additional understanding that Marv really had no choice.

THE ESSENCE OF THIS APPROACH

Mike makes the best of a bad situation regarding the recruitment need at the same time that he tries to motivate and caution Marv for the future.

B. Mike can tell Marv that he — Marv — has failed to demonstrate the required initiative regarding the recruitment need and, as a further example, regarding most of his duties calling for the proper planning.

Mike then tells Marv that he — Mike — is going to assume Marv's long-range planning duty (already neglected) this one time by placing the requisition himself. He then tells Marv that the next time that Marv fails to show the proper initiative and drive regarding *any* of his duties, this will be cause for a reconsideration of Marv's fitness for his job.

THE ESSENCE OF THIS APPROACH

Mike dramatizes to Marv his failure to do the right thing, embarrasses him for it and cautions him not to neglect again either his long-range planning duties or any other responsibilities involving initiative and drive.

ADAPTING THESE SOLUTIONS TO YOUR OWN WORK

When a foreman (or other assistant) is supposed to engage in long-range planning it's best to set up the kinds of controls which will bring to your attention — earlier rather than later — his tendencies to neglect such planning. Then, as soon as it becomes obvious that he is neglecting or about to neglect such planning, remedy the defect at once (even if you have to assume some of *his* duties yourself), emphasize the need to assume the necessary initiative and make sure he understands that he has no choice.

SITUATION NUMBER 50 — The lack of initiative and drive regarding the assessment and improvement of the morale of his assistants.

INCIDENT

Matt Raffin is in charge of ten office workers; Mel Sacks, his boss, has often emphasized to his assistants that they must always know how their men feel about their jobs, the company and their immediate superiors. One day one of the company's best clerks, working under Matt, gave notice that he was quitting. Nothing could persuade him to change his mind.

During the exit interview the personnel department discovered, as substantiated by their further inquiries among Matt's men, that the employee who had quit had long been dissatisfied with certain aspects of his job and with being passed over during the last two salary reviews.

Not once had Matt told Mel anything about that employee's attitudes toward the company or his job.

ALTERNATE SOLUTIONS

A. Mel can call Matt in and talk to him along these lines:

- You've just lost one of your best workers.
- Investigation reveals that he'd long been dissatisfied with certain aspects of his job.
- You've never spoken to me about him.
- What did you know about his morale and what did you do about it?

THE ESSENCE OF THIS APPROACH

Mel lays it on the line to Matt as concisely and as pointedly as possible, throwing the burden on Matt to defend himself.

B. Mel can tell Matt what the personnel department told him, point out that Matt had never reported to Mel on that employee's morale and tell him that he has therefore neglected one of his more important duties (so often stressed by Mel): that of constantly assessing morale and doing something about low morale.

Mel further points out that this is an indication of a lack of drive on Matt's part which may be simply symptomatic of Matt's attitude toward *all* of his job.

THE ESSENCE OF THIS APPROACH

Mel charges Matt with the failure to meet one of his important responsibilities and puts him on notice that the greater failing may be a lack of drive on Matt's part which, if repeatedly manifested, could lead to undesirable consequences.

C. Mel can sit down with Matt and say to him:

- You've neglected one of your duties — assessing morale.
- Why did you do so, and what are you going to do to prevent this shortcoming in the future?
- Is this failure simply attributable to your attitude about this one duty or shall I interpret it as a symptom of your general lack of drive?
- Let's see whether you can't convince me by your future actions that this was only one isolated case of your failure to take the initiative.

THE ESSENCE OF THIS APPROACH

Mel sandwiches criticism in between optimism and positivism, without in any way mitigating Matt's failure.

ADAPTING THESE SOLUTIONS TO YOUR OWN WORK

When you check up on your assistants to see whether they are consistently meeting their responsibilities, don't overlook the way in which they attend to some of their less tangible duties like assessing morale and acting on it. Whenever you discover that they are not meeting this duty properly or have already neglected it, pinpoint the failure and take necessary steps to prevent its recurrence. Don't neglect the opportunity to use that kind of failure as a springboard for emphasizing the broader need for exercising initiative and drive in general.

SITUATION NUMBER 51 — The lack of initiative and drive regarding the older employee whose productivity has deteriorated.

INCIDENT

Ab Caldwell was promoted to head one of the company's inside sales divisions. He supervised, among others, Byron D'Amato, who had been the company's technical specialist for that division's product line for many years. Byron had been yielding less and less productivity over the last few years, and was close to the earliest age at which the company paid any retirement pension.

Ab's boss, Norbert Eckstein, had given Ab a free hand to reorganize the division and make recommendations regarding specific individuals working in it. Norbert began to notice that Byron's results, as reflected in Norbert's appropriate non-bypassing supervision, were steadily getting poorer. Ab had made no move to request that something be done about Byron.

ALTERNATE SOLUTIONS

A. Norbert can ask Ab to sit down with him and review all of Ab's assistants, without mentioning any one of them by name. If Ab's report on Byron is a satisfactory one, Norbert can point out his own findings and ask Ab why the discrepancy. If, however, Ab volunteers the kind of information that Norbert already has, he can ask Ab what he wants to do about it.

In either case, Norbert can appropriately ask Ab why he didn't take the proper initiative, either to arrive at the facts or to act properly on them.

THE ESSENCE OF THIS APPROACH

Norbert gives Ab an opportunity to come up with a belated initiative regarding Byron, thus purging himself of the possible claim that he lacked it. Norbert can still reprove Ab if this becomes necessary.

B. Norbert can tell Ab exactly how Byron has deteriorated, showing him that there was no improvement under Ab's new job. Norbert can then ask Ab why he, Norbert, shouldn't come to the conclusion that Ab has exercised no initiative in remedying the situation.

If Ab cannot satisfy Norbert to the contrary, Norbert can indicate his displeasure and urge Ab not only to take the necessary action in Byron's case but also to make an effort to increase and improve his initiative and drive in general.

THE ESSENCE OF THIS APPROACH

Norbert comes right to the point of his inferences, but still gives Ab a chance to disprove Norbert's conclusions.

ADAPTING THESE SOLUTIONS TO YOUR OWN WORK

One of the most common examples of an assistant's failure to exercise proper initiative and drive is his reluctance to take steps which might lead to making an older employee unhappy. Such thinking, no matter how noble, can lead only to lesser profitability.

You must insist that your assistants be constantly alert to the productivity of *all* of their men. If they detect that any of them are sliding irremediably, they must recommend that such employees be taken away from duties which stand in the way of someone else filling them better. Every effort can then be made to minimize the harm to the slider, but nothing must interfere with initiative leading to profit.

SITUATION NUMBER 52 — The manager who lacks initiative and drive regarding efforts to find and encourage worthy assistants capable of upgrading.

INCIDENT

Dana Fallon is in charge of a large segment of the company's office. His boss is Vito Galiano. One of Dana's supervisors has a heart attack and must suddenly stop work — permanently. Vito asks Dana whom he plans to put into the vacant position. Dana says he has no assistant other than another supervisor already doing a good and necessary job in another section who is capable of filling the empty spot.

ALTERNATE SOLUTIONS

A. Vito can ask the personnel department to start looking around for a potential candidate for the vacancy, either from within the company or outside of it. He can then tell Dana that he'll have to cover the unsupervised section as best he can until a new man is found.

He also points out to Dana that he has been remiss in not having someone ready to fill the spot, expressing the hope that this will not happen again.

THE ESSENCE OF THIS APPROACH

Vito takes the necessary steps at once to fill the vacancy and cover the vacated section with the proper supervision, while pointing out that Dana has failed to show the necessary initiative and had better not be guilty of it again.

B. Vito can sit down at once with Dana and tell him:

- Contact the personnel department at once and get the job filled as soon as possible.
- Meanwhile, cover the vacated section adequately.
- When you've made arrangements for that, let me know at once, so we can talk some more.

When Dana reports that he has taken the necessary steps, Vito sits down with him again and says:

- An important responsibility that goes with your job is always to maintain the proper level of initiative and drive.
- One aspect of this duty is constantly to be looking for and upgrading, without any promises, assistants capable of assuming higher positions in the company.

- You didn't do this, with the results we both know about.
- I'm confident that you will rectify this situation.

THE ESSENCE OF THIS APPROACH

Vito, after taking care of the immediate emergency, spells out exactly where Dana has been remiss, both generically and specifically. He then expresses his positive feeling that Dana will overcome that previous weakness.

C. Vito can ask Dana to review with him at once the men who work for him. Following this up with appropriate personal interviews — Dana being present — Vito can decide on a worthy replacement for the separated employee. If any training is necessary, Vito sees to it that it is accomplished.

Vito then points out to Dana that had he exercised the proper initiative the current problem wouldn't have arisen.

THE ESSENCE OF THIS APPROACH

Vito dramatizes to Dana the effectiveness of the initiative in question at the same time that he solves the problem caused by Dana's lack of drive.

ADAPTING THESE SOLUTIONS TO YOUR OWN WORK

It's wise to tell all of your management assistants that their positions call for initiative and drive in general. To illustrate your point, tell them about the need to always be on the alert for men who can be upgraded in case of an emergency. You might also help your assistants to plan for a continuing program for such upgrading, without promise of promotion. It's also wise to ask your assistants to submit actual prospect names to you from time to time.

If, however, it turns out that a vacancy occurs in one of your assistants' sections for which there is no valid candidate:

- Attend to the emergency at once.
- Point out to the culprit not only his specific failure but also his general lack of initiative and drive.

- End this remonstrance on a positive note, but make it clear that you mean business.

SITUATION NUMBER 53 — The manager who lacks initiative and drive regarding the discipline of employees.

INCIDENT

Dom Hallowell had been an hourly employee. He had been promoted to foreman because he had demonstrated his ability and willingness to fill the vacancy which had been created in his own department.

For years, Dom had been very friendly with one of his fellow-employees, Emil Ingram. Before Dom was given the new job he had been told by the superintendent, Gil Jacobson, that a foreman cannot fraternize with one of his workers (either outside or inside the plant) and still be able to criticize him where necessary. Dom had indicated that he would talk to Emil, explain the situation to him and reduce their relationship to the same one that Dom had with all of his other men.

But Gil has heard the other men complaining that Dom was continually playing favorites with Emil, that he was always joking with him on the job and that they were often seen at night, in a local tavern. Gil has brought this to Dom's attention and the latter has each time either denied the allegation or promised to reform.

ALTERNATE SOLUTIONS

A.   Gil can tell Dom that he — Dom — has shown a marked lack of initiative in doing what he had been told to do and had promised to do. He can then tell Dom that as a result of this and Gil's conviction that Dom will never do what he must in that regard, he is transfering Dom to another section, where his continued fraternization can do less harm.

THE ESSENCE OF THIS APPROACH

Gil solves the problem resulting from the lack of initiative and gives Dom a chance to prove that he can demonstrate his general initiative in another department where the problem with Emil doesn't exist.

B. Gil can transfer Emil out of Dom's department and tell Dom why he has done so, cautioning him to keep his relationship with Emil strictly outside of the plant.

THE ESSENCE OF THIS APPROACH

Emil is removed from Dom as a temptation for Dom to disobey Gil's instructions. Dom has another chance to prove that he can take the proper initiative regarding Emil in the new situation.

C. Gil can warn Dom that he has a last chance to show the proper initiative by obeying Gil's instructions regarding Emil. He can tell Dom that the next time that he gets evidence that Dom is favoring Emil — for whatever reason — he may have to consider removing Dom from the ranks of foremen.

THE ESSENCE OF THIS APPROACH

Gil sticks to the basic issues of initiative and obedience. If Dom cannot tear himself away from Emil this must mean that Dom has certain basic weaknesses which would demonstrate themselves in other connections and could hurt his ability to be an effective foreman in general.

ADAPTING THESE SOLUTIONS TO YOUR OWN WORK

In general, it's wise to appoint hourly employees into management positions outside of the one where they themselves functioned. In all cases of intent to promote a non-management man to management, be sure to convince the man that he cannot and must not permit personal friendship to interfere with his job.

10

How to Handle
The Unreasonable Boss

In the following situations notice how the assistant maintains the proper show of respect and appreciation for his boss while insisting on his own right to be treated reasonably and fairly, with respect and dignity. Notice also that the assistant recognizes and acknowledges that his boss may be under pressure when he seems to be acting unreasonably, and makes allowances for this.

SITUATION NUMBER 54 — The unreasonable boss who speaks to you disrespectfully.

INCIDENT

Orlando Zenner works for Gus Kellerman. Orlando is a very conscientious, loyal and competent assistant — and Gus knows it.

Gus is also very competent and hardworking, but he has a short temper and is under great pressure. Lately Gus has been speaking sarcastically and rudely to Orlando.

ALTERNATE SOLUTIONS

A. The next time that Gus speaks that way to Orlando, Orlando can wait until Gus has finished what he has to say, tell him he wants to think about it and excuse himself to go back to his own office.

Then, unless the matter is one of extreme importance, Orlando should simply not do what Gus has asked him to do while speaking that way. If Gus asks him why he didn't attend to the matter, Orlando can say that he hasn't been able to come to the necessary decision because he didn't fully understand what Gus had in mind: Gus must have been under strain because he didn't address Orlando calmly, which resulted in Orlando's confusion.

THE ESSENCE OF THIS APPROACH

Orlando doesn't directly tell Gus that he — Gus — spoke disrespectfully to Orlando. Orlando simply refuses to act on instructions issued disrespectfully, and implies that, when asked.

B. Orlando can wait until Gus has finished talking and then say something like: "Are you annoyed with me about anything?" If Gus says that he isn't and asks why the question, Orlando can say (in his own words): "Well, you talked to me in a way which isn't normal for you when you're satisfied with my work, and I was wondering what was wrong."

THE ESSENCE OF THIS APPROACH

Orlando brings to Gus's direct attention that he is not talking to Orlando the way he wants to be addressed, being subtle about it.

C. The next time that Gus speaks to him in a manner which seems disrespectful, Orlando can simply say to Gus: "Do you mean to treat me disrespectfully by the way in which you said that?" Depending on how Gus replies, Orlando can then say something like:

- If you have no respect for me, I'd like to know why, so I can earn it.
- If you do respect me, why do I get the feeling that you don't?"

THE ESSENCE OF THIS APPROACH

Orlando confronts Gus directly with what's bothering him and gives Gus the chance to confirm or deny Orlando's opinion of the matter of respect.

ADAPTING THESE SOLUTIONS TO YOUR OWN WORK

You must be sure that you are competent, hard-working, loyal and effective in the work that your boss assigns to you. Once you have that confidence you have a right to expect and insist that you be treated respectfully.

If you get the feeling that your boss is talking or acting disrespectfully to you, try being subtle in bringing this to his attention. If subtlety doesn't work, call your complaint to his attention directly.

If he still treats you disrespectfully you have to decide whether you want to take it. If you opt for not accepting it, at least give him a chance to turn over a new leaf on the avowed statement that if he doesn't you'll have to ask for a transfer.

SITUATION NUMBER 55 — The unreasonable boss who takes too long to tell you things.

INCIDENT

Hector Lakin works for Nat MacLean. Whenever Nat wants Hector to undertake a new or different task, he takes a long time to explain what he wants done. Usually Hector gets the complete picture during the first quarter of the explanation; then, when Nat has stopped talking he sets a deadline for the completion of the job which is made more difficult because Hector can't get started on it until Nat finishes talking.

ALTERNATE SOLUTIONS

A. Hector can wait until Nat finishes talking and ask for an extension of the deadline time. If Nat wants to know why, Hector can say that the time has to run from the time that Nat has finished giving Hector his instructions, which is *now,* and that there isn't enough time from *now* on to complete the job when Nat says he wants it.

THE ESSENCE OF THIS APPROACH

Hector throws the onus on Nat to become aware of the time factor without directly mentioning Hector's feeling that Nat talked too long.

B. When Nat finally excuses Hector, Hector can enter on his daily report the exact time that Nat took for the explanation and indicate that he — Hector — resumed his duties only *after* the end of that time. Hector can then indicate that the time taken for the explanation meant that he had to postpone one or more of his other duties.

THE ESSENCE OF THIS APPROACH

Hector again acts subtly, except that this time he relates his reaction about time to other duties which had to be postponed because of the situation.

ADAPTING THESE SOLUTIONS TO YOUR OWN WORK

Your time is valuable. If your boss is unreasonable in how he uses it you must find a way to prevent him from doing this without offending him by telling him that he is unnecessarily detailed in explaining things to you.

Every time he takes longer than you need to tell you what he wants you to do, find some tactful, subtle way of calling this to his attention.

SITUATION NUMBER 56 — The unreasonable boss who resents suggestions or facts reflecting his weakness or mistake.

INCIDENT

Herman Nass is responsible for a large quantity of steady paperwork. He has six assistants.

When one of his assistants is absent Herman can't meet the daily needs for processing the documents without doing the actual work of the absent assistant by himself. When he does so, not only does the quality of the work deteriorate for his whole department but the quantity is even diminished and he is still behind schedule.

Herman has repeatedly explained this to his boss, Irwin O'Donnell, and has asked him to authorize another position, claiming that even with no absences the additional cost could be justified. Irwin has refused to put the request in for next year's budget, saying that he wants to keep costs down.

Irwin's boss called Irwin in one day and reamed him for the quality of the paperwork from Irwin's department as well as for the timeliness of the flow. Irwin then calls Herman in and, in turn, reams him for the same shortcoming.

ALTERNATE SOLUTIONS

A. If Herman is fairly secure in his job, knows that he is doing the best he can and feels that it's futile to protest that the problem was not caused by him, he can simply listen to Irwin, express his regrets, promise to do better next time and not mention the real reason for the difficulty.

THE ESSENCE OF THIS APPROACH

Herman lets Irwin blow off steam and avoids an unpleasant encounter which would do no good.

B. Herman can ask Irwin whether he knows why Herman's results were what they were. He tries to get Irwin to realize that the cause of the problem is the failure to have the additional person he had requested, and asks Irwin to put in an amended budget request to prevent a recurrence.

THE ESSENCE OF THIS APPROACH

Herman tries to get Irwin to initiate the justification that Herman feels for himself and uses the situation as a springboard for a renewed request for the help he needs.

C. Herman can say to Irwin:

- I'm sorry that your boss is displeased with my work.

- I cannot permit anybody to blame me for something that is not my fault.
- I urge you to reconsider your judgment of my role in this unfortunate situation.
- I'll still continue to do the best I can under these impossible conditions but I won't be happy doing it if you keep on thinking that my work is less professional than I know it is.

THE ESSENCE OF THIS APPROACH

Herman lets Irwin know in no uncertain terms that he will not treat unjustified accusations lightly, although he will live with that condition if he has to.

ADAPTING THESE SOLUTIONS TO YOUR OWN WORK

Be sure that you are the best assistant that your boss can possibly have. Always do a first-rate job. Where you know that you are being kept from achieving your maximum/optimum potential, tell your boss what you'd like him to do for you.

If he refuses to do this, choose your own way of telling him but either disregard his unjust criticisms or stand up to him in the face of them, depending on what makes you most comfortable.

SITUATION NUMBER 57 — The unreasonable boss who piles too much work on you.

INCIDENT

Monroe Worms is one of several engineering supervisors reporting to Iz Rakoff. Monroe manages his draftsmen very efficiently and turns out more work of a high quality than any of the other supervisors.

Iz has a tendency to pile more work on Monroe than even he can turn out in keeping with his high standards. Part of this is due to Iz's awareness of the deficiencies of some of his other assistants.

ALTERNATE SOLUTIONS

A. Monroe can accept all of the work that Iz asks him to do, but each time he gets a new assignment — tell Iz that he — Monroe — can make no promise regarding deadline dates.

Monroe then schedules the new work according to his own judgment of priorities and emphasizes quality results without worrying about when the work will be finished.

THE ESSENCE OF THIS APPROACH

Monroe doesn't have to state or imply any gripes and still maintains his usual high standards of results.

B.   Each time that Iz asks Monroe to undertake another job, if Monroe is already fully loaded he can say to Iz: "Which of my present assignments would you like me to stop in order to accommodate this new one?"

THE ESSENCE OF THIS APPROACH

Monroe throws the burden on Iz of deciding priorities, thus demonstrating a willingness to cooperate without assuming an impossible commitment.

ADAPTING THESE SOLUTIONS TO YOUR OWN WORK

Don't let your boss pile more work on you than you can handle with your normal standards. Either tell him that you'll do it according to your own schedule or let him set the schedule.

11

How to Handle
The Manager
Who Communicates Ineffectively

In the following situations notice how easy it is to communicate without regard to its proper understanding and receptivity. Note that with a modicum of care a manager can turn a random dissemination, little understood or greatly misinterpreted, into a message which is received, understood and acted on exactly as it is intended.

SITUATION NUMBER 58 — The manager who communicates ineffectively because he relies on oral communications when he should use written communications.

INCIDENT

Adam Sago is in charge of shipping. He reports to Zeke Tanner.

The sales department has been complaining to Zeke that a number of shipments to important customers have been delayed, others have been short and still others have been wrong in their makeup. Zeke promises to investigate.

He discovers that Adam is in the habit of telling his shipping clerks — orally — what materials are to go where, when and to whom. The clerks, it is true, make note of what Adam tells them in writing. It is done, however, in an informal way.

ALTERNATE SOLUTIONS

A. Zeke can design a form for the written communication of all shipping instructions by Adam to his clerks and insist that the form be used all the time.

THE ESSENCE OF THIS APPROACH

Zeke simply puts a stop to Adam's undesirable communication practice and insists that this particular information be transmitted in writing.

B. Zeke can tell Adam that there have been a number of complaints about shipments and ask Adam to look into it and report to him on the causes. If Adam doesn't come up with the reason that his shipping clerks are misinterpreting his instructions because they are oral, Zeke can then point this out and tell Adam to use written instructions thenceforth.

THE ESSENCE OF THIS APPROACH

Zeke gives Adam an opportunity to get the message on his own, thus making him assume his real management responsibility in solving the problem himself.

C. Zeke can ask Adam to collect as many as possible of the written notes made by his clerks in the last few weeks and bring them to Zeke for an analysis and discussion. Zeke can then try to trace the relationships between customer complaints, Adam's memory of what he told the clerks and the actual writings they made. Zeke can then try to get Adam to see for himself the dangers in oral communications not only in that situation but also in other equally important situations.

THE ESSENCE OF THIS APPROACH

Zeke tries to get Adam to understand the basic concept of using written communications in all important situations.

ADAPTING THESE SOLUTIONS TO YOUR OWN WORK

Whenever your assistants are required to communicate important matters to their people, the surest way to guarantee that written communications will be used when desirable is to provide them with the proper forms; then, whenever there is an error of any significance related to such communications, the field of inquiry can be narrowed down to how only one type of document was executed.

When a form is not appropriate, simply insist that any communication of importance can be accurate and complete only if it is written properly.

SITUATION NUMBER 59 — The manager who communicates ineffectively because he is careless in his semantics.

INCIDENT

Armand Uzzi, like the rest of his peers in the company, has a budget which allows him to reward his foremen financially for their unusual results at the end of each year. Armand has been calling this incentive "profit sharing," although the company has put no official label on it.

Clarence Walden is Armand's boss. He is reviewing the results of Armand's foremen's work for the year and doesn't understand why more of them don't merit and/or receive extra compensation.

Clarence asks around and discovers that some of the foremen have this attitude:

- I can work very hard and my men can produce exceptionally well, but someone else in the company can cause a lessening of profit and deprive me of my share in what I could otherwise get.
- Therefore, why should I break my back to try to earn what someone else can take away from me?

Clarence also finds out that Armand's description of the plan to his men is not accurate.

ALTERNATE SOLUTIONS

A. Clarence can call Armand in and tell him:

- The company's plan revolves around *profitability* (contribution to profit) and not *profit* (the total difference between company-wide income and company-wide costs).
- He should explain to his foremen that each of them will share in his *contribution* to profit regardless of whether there is a profit and of how other foremen affect profit.

THE ESSENCE OF THIS APPROACH

Clarence helps Armand to clarify his own semantics as a prelude to making them clear to his foremen.

B. Clarence can tell Armand:

- Your men are misunderstanding our plan because you are calling it *profit sharing* when it is actually a reward for their *contribution* to profit.
- Not only should you explain this to them carefully, but you should watch the same thing in other communications to your men.
- Make sure that when you use a word which is capable of more than one interpretation you surround it with other words which will clarify the *exact* meaning *you* want it to have.

THE ESSENCE OF THIS APPROACH

Clarence not only corrects Armand's weakness in the given situation but tries to get him into the habit of being more careful in his semantics in general.

ADAPTING THESE SOLUTIONS TO YOUR OWN WORK

Every manager must communicate with his assistants as well as with others, all the time. Effective communications are the number one problem in the business world. The most serious cause of ineffective communications is sloppy semantics.

Since in English (as well as in other languages) a word can have more than one *correct* meaning, you want to make sure that when you use it to others you make perfectly clear *which* meaning *you* have in mind.

You can do this by surrounding the word with others which give it *your* unmistakable meaning; you can ask questions to reveal whether *your* meaning prevailed, or you can use a different word (or expression) which permits no misinterpretation.

SITUATION NUMBER 60 — The manager who communicates ineffectively because he leaves gaps in his development of the communication.

INCIDENT

Ernie Adams has urged his foremen to pay continuing strict attention to preventive maintenance. Ernie has explained all facets of that managerial activity to them.

Ernie finds that the equipment in Hans Baird's department — the same machinery as exists in the other departments — breaks down more often than the equipment in the other departments. On investigation, Ernie learns that Hans' inspection is just as good as is the inspection in the other departments, but that Hans has neglected to stress to his men the proper use of the equipment to avoid breakdowns.

ALTERNATE SOLUTIONS

A. Ernie can point out to Hans:

- Your equipment breaks down more than does that of the others.
- Your inspection is satisfactory.
- You aren't explaining adequately to your men the proper use of the equipment, and that is causing them to be either unaware or careless of the effects on breakdowns of the way in which they use the machinery.

THE ESSENCE OF THIS APPROACH

Ernie re-emphasizes to Hans his need to pay careful attention to the one area of preventive maintenance where Hans has been remiss.

B. Ernie can reissue his instructions to Hans, first in writing and then orally, stressing these points:

- Preventive maintenance is an important part of your duties.
- It consists of two major types of activities: periodic inspection and proper use of equipment.

Ernie can then tell Hans where he has been weak and urge him to convey effectively to his men how to use the machinery in order to avoid breakdowns.

THE ESSENCE OF THIS APPROACH

Ernie goes back to basics, thus enforcing Hans's understanding of what he must do, say and follow up on.

C. Ernie can call together all of his foremen and tell them:

- Most of you are enforcing our preventive maintenance program properly.
- Some of you are less effective in this than others.
- Let me repeat my instructions regarding preventive maintenance.
- Any questions?
- Here is a reissue of the written instructions.
- When you talk to your men about preventive maintenance you must emphasize not only their prompt reporting to you of potential or actual breakdowns, but also how they are to use the equipment in order to minimize breakdowns.
- In general, whenever you have to explain anything to your men, don't take anything for granted. Leave no gaps in the development of your communications.

THE ESSENCE OF THIS APPROACH

Ernie takes advantage of the situation to reaffirm to *all* of his men his wishes not only regarding preventive maintenance, but also regarding one of the greatest weaknesses in effective communications.

ADAPTING THESE SOLUTIONS TO YOUR OWN WORK

When you communicate to your assistants, make sure that *you* leave no gaps in the development of your wishes regarding what you want them to do. Even that is not enough, however. Train your men in how *they* should effectively communicate without gaps and, where a management duty is important enough to warrant it, spell the development out for them — step by step — both in writing and orally. Then urge them to follow that sequence and make no omissions.

As regards preventive maintenance, make sure to issue to them a complete set of instructions on how their men are to *use* their equipment in order to minimize breakdowns.

SITUATION NUMBER 61 — The manager who communicates ineffectively because he is unwilling to be forceful regarding orders or instructions.

INCIDENT

Ivan Edelman has told his supervisors that he wants them to crack down on the prevailing practice of their employees in getting to their desks late in the morning and leaving them early in the afternoon at the end of the work day. He has said that he wants them to see to it that all of their people are punctual at both times unless they have valid excuses.

Ivan has been spot-checking adherence to these instructions and has discovered that the people working for one of the supervisors — Justin Callahan — generally do not conform to the stated policy.

Ivan asks around and comes to the conclusion that Justin has only halfheartedly told his people about the rule, doesn't always check up on whether they are prompt and, when he does find that they are not, either doesn't criticize them or admonishes them too gently.

ALTERNATE SOLUTIONS

A. Ivan can call Justin in and talk to him as follows:

- What is your assessment of how your people are following the promptness rule?

- Why are some of them not following it consistently?
- What do you intend to do about it?

THE ESSENCE OF THIS APPROACH

Ivan gives Justin another chance to be forceful in his communications regarding the rule, without revealing that Justin has already been negligent.

B. Ivan can talk to Justin as follows:

- You will remember the rule I issued about promptness.
- I've checked up all around and find that your people are lacking in that respect more than the employees reporting to the other supervisors.
- Perhaps you haven't been as forceful in your instructions to them as you should have been.
- I want you to restate the rule to them in no uncertain terms.
- I want you then to regularly check up on their compliance.
- If there are still offenders, handle them in the usual way for those who consistently violate company policy.
- If you can't seem to get one or more of your people to obey, come to me and we'll see what has to be done.

THE ESSENCE OF THIS APPROACH

Ivan lays it on the line for Justin. He tells him where the weakness is, gives Justin a chance to save face and then spells out exactly how Justin is to be forceful in his communications on this matter.

ADAPTING THESE SOLUTIONS TO YOUR OWN WORK

When you issue a rule or order to your assistants, which they must in turn convey to their own people, make sure that they understand that that rule *must* be enforced. If one or more of your supervisors seems not to be enforcing a particular rule, find out how he feels about it. He may either be lukewarm to the concept (in which case you may have to heat him up some) or he may not want to appear to be too harsh to his people (in which case you should insist that he enforce the rules).

SITUATION NUMBER 62 — The manager who communicates ineffectively because he issues too many communications.

INCIDENT

Marshall D'Angelo is in charge of four office supervisors.

Whenever Marshall sends a directive to all four of them with a copy for each, he sends a copy to his boss, Warren Ziehl, as well.

Warren began to get the impression that Marshall was issuing too many directives and sending out messages too frequently. Warren also concluded that a number of the writings were mutually contradictory.

Warren checked around and discovered that for the most part, Marshall's supervisors were confused and upset by the barrage.

ALTERNATE SOLUTIONS

A. Warren can tell Marshall that he is sending out too many directives, that this is resulting in confusion and demoralization among the supervisors and that Marshall is to proceed, from now on, as follows:

- If he is faced with a real emergency, best met by a written directive, he should send it out on his own.
- In all other cases, he is to clear it with Warren before he sends out a directive.

THE ESSENCE OF THIS APPROACH

Warren puts a direct and immediate stop to the undesirable practice, while still allowing Marshall to exercise his discretion, explaining to him why. He can then follow up, through *his* copies, to see whether Marshall is meeting the policy.

Warren puts a direct and immediate stop to the undesirable

practice, while still allowing Marshall to exercise his directive authority in a limited area.

B.   Warren can ask Marshall to cut down on the number of directives, explaining to him why. He can then follow up, through *his* copies, to see whether Marshall is meeting the policy.

THE ESSENCE OF THIS APPROACH

Warren leaves it up to Marshall to solve the problem by himself, thus retaining full authority.

C.   Warren can call Marshall in each time Warren receives a copy of a directive which he thinks unnecessary. Warren can then react to it as though he were one of the supervisors involved, telling Marshall what effect the directive has had on him — Warren. He then asks Marshall whether it isn't reasonable to assume that his — Warren's — reaction is the same as that of the supervisors.

Warren can then ask Marshall to do the right thing about the situation, leaving the method to Marshall.

THE ESSENCE OF THIS APPROACH

Warren brings the problem to Marshall's attention on a per each basis, thus making him more aware of the need to solve it.

ADAPTING THESE SOLUTIONS TO YOUR OWN WORK

You must keep yourself informed of the number and nature of the written communications your assistants are issuing. If it seems that they are sending out too many directives, especially when they are sometimes mutually contradictory, you should find a way of bringing this to their attention — preferably tactfully and subtly; then you must see to it that the practice is modified accordingly.

12

How to Handle
The Manager
Who Supervises His Assistants
Inadequately or Improperly

In the following situations notice how the responsibility of supervision is first clearly spelled out, then its importance is stressed and finally, the particular practice of undesirable supervision is pinpointed, brought to the manager's attention and presented to him as a problem that has to be properly solved.

SITUATION NUMBER 63 — The manager who supervises his assistants inadequately or improperly by spending too much time in his office.

INCIDENT

Marlin Worrell is a production foreman. His superintendent is Salwyn Wales.

On his rounds Salwyn has noticed that a number of Marlin's men are apparently less productive than they are capable of being and that Marlin is usually in his office when Salwyn comes by.

While in his office Marlin is busily shuffling papers.

ALTERNATE SOLUTIONS

A. Salwyn can simply tell Marlin that he'll have to schedule his time between his paperwork and his obligation to move about among his men more effectively. Salwyn can point out his findings and emphasize that inadequate or improper worker productivity is costly and can be prevented mostly by adequate and proper supervision.

THE ESSENCE OF THIS APPROACH

Salwyn insists on Marlin's devoting the right amount of time to this most important duty.

B. Salwyn can make arrangements for Marlin to take care of his paperwork at prescribed times and in a prescribed place other than an office specifically assigned to Marlin. Salwyn then takes away Marlin's present office and tells him that:

- His prime job is to be out on the floor with the men, supervising them properly.
- His paperwork is to be done in that special place assigned to him for that work at specified times not cutting in too much on his physical supervision time.

THE ESSENCE OF THIS APPROACH

Salwyn removes the temptation for Marlin to spend time in an office. He makes provision for only essential paperwork and encourages more floor time.

ADAPTING THESE SOLUTIONS TO YOUR OWN WORK

A foreman's job is primarily to be physically present among his men whenever they are working. Whatever additional duties he has should be kept to a minimum, at least during the shift.

If a foreman has an office for himself or other space which he is authorized to use on a regular basis, he is tempted to be *there* rather than where he should be.

SITUATION NUMBER 64 — The manager who supervises his assistants inadequately or improperly by neglecting certain areas of his responsibility.

INCIDENT

Sanford Gallo is the company's office manager. He has many departments and assistants to control. He works under Vince Halstead.

One of Sanford's responsibilities is the rather large company mailroom, under a supervisor. Many of the company's department heads complain to Vince that the pickup and delivery of mail — both intraoffice and with the outside — is excessively slow. Vince investigates and discovers that this is true. Further inquiry reveals that Sanford visits the mailroom very infrequently and hasn't checked up on its functioning in considerable time.

ALTERNATE SOLUTIONS

A. Vince can ask Sanford to make a survey with him for several days, actually visiting the mailroom on a spot basis, noting pickup and delivery times and otherwise tracing the flow of mail and other items to be transmitted.

If Sanford comes to the same conclusions as Vince, the latter can ask Sanford what he thinks is the best way of remedying the situation, leading Sanford to the conclusion that the mail area needs better supervision by him.

THE ESSENCE OF THIS APPROACH

Vince lets Sanford come to his own assessment of both the problem and its solution, thus assuring readier acceptance of the need for better supervision.

B. Vince can turn over to Sanford all of the complaints that have been made to him — Vince — and ask Sanford to look into them and report back to him both his own findings and his suggestions on what, if anything, should be done about them.

THE ESSENCE OF THIS APPROACH

Vince gets Sanford involved in even more basic responsibilities: people have complained to me about your bailiwick; that's your baby; you take care of it and let me know what you intend to do about it.

C. Vince can investigate the complaints to see whether

they are valid. If they are, he can then spot-check the degree to which Sanford supervises the mailroom.

If he finds this inadequate, he then calls Sanford in and says to him:

- Here are the complaints I've received about the mail system.
- I've investigated them and found them to be accurate.
- I've also checked up on your supervisory schedule and find you not visiting the mailroom sufficiently and not checking up enough on the pickup and delivery throughout the company.
- What's your explanation for this?

If Sanford can present a valid reason for his failure to properly supervise the mail activities, Vince can do what has to be done. If on the other hand Sanford has no valid justification for his shortcoming, Vince can urge him to rectify it and caution him on the seriousness of his not doing so.

THE ESSENCE OF THIS APPROACH

Vince presents Sanford with verified complaints, both his own and those of others, and gives Sanford a chance to explain them. If Sanford cannot do so, Vince then reminds Sanford of his relevant responsibility and motivates him to meet it better in the future.

ADAPTING THESE SOLUTIONS TO YOUR OWN WORK

You must make it your responsibility to know whether your assistants are neglecting their supervisory duties. This you do best by spot-checking. If you discover their lacks through the complaints of others, you'd best check up and take speedy action.

SITUATION NUMBER 65 — The manager who supervises his assistants inadequately or improperly by making too superficial an examination.

INCIDENT

Saul Inman is the foreman of a component assembly line. Terence Jacy is his superintendent.

The foreman whose production begins on receipt of the components from Saul's department complains to Saul that too many of the components received are defective and can't be used. When Saul denies the validity of the complaint, the other foreman asks Saul to come with him to Terence. Saul refuses and the other foreman says he's going to Terence alone, which he does.

Terence watches Saul more carefully than he had in the past and discovers that Saul concentrates his inspection of the completed components on appearance only without applying the other tests available to him.

ALTERNATE SOLUTIONS

A. Terence can ask Saul to spend time with him in the inspection process, so that the two of them can do the same thing simultaneously. If in the process Terence finds that Saul is not being as careful as Terence would be, Terence can ask Saul why he does only what he does rather than being more detailed.

If Saul doesn't come up with a satisfactory answer, Terence can then simply tell Saul what he wants him to do and that he — Terence — will be checking up on whether Saul is complying.

THE ESSENCE OF THIS APPROACH

Terence dramatizes the situation involved to Saul, and gives Saul an opportunity to rectify it himself. If Saul then doesn't respond properly, Terence can still rely on his authority.

B. Terence can ask Saul:

- Why he didn't want to accompany the other foreman to see him. If the answer is not acceptable, that then becomes an auxiliary matter for Terence to discuss.
- Whether he agrees that there are too many components leaving his department improperly completed. If Saul's

answer isn't satisfactory, that's yet another matter for correction.

- Why he doesn't use all of the tests available to him. Here, too, an unacceptable reply must be taken up.

Terence then does what he must to convince Saul that he simply has to supervise the end product more carefully and that he — Terence — will know whether Saul is doing this.

THE ESSENCE OF THIS APPROACH

Terence uses the incident as a springboard for more than one management problem. He sees to it that Saul understands the need to supervise more carefully, but he also takes steps to strengthen Saul's general managerial habits.

ADAPTING THESE SOLUTIONS TO YOUR OWN WORK

Your assistants must supervise everything that they are responsible for, and must do so with the necessary degree of thoroughness. Either an activity must be supervised well or it needn't be supervised at all.

While it is true that some activities take more time than others and may require more frequent investigations, any activity which requires supervision must be supervised with sufficient completeness.

SITUATION NUMBER 66 — The manager who supervises his assistants inadequately or improperly by acting too officiously while moving about.

INCIDENT

Bruce Kaltman is a foreman, reporting to Cole Lambert. Cole has observed Bruce in his rounds among the workers and has heard some rumblings, leading to Cole's conclusion that Bruce's bearing and manner leave something to be desired.

Cole judges that the men feel that Bruce is snooping with a negative attitude, as if to say that he's the boss and the employees had better quake in their boots when he's around.

ALTERNATE SOLUTIONS

A. Cole can ask Bruce whether he has any idea of the re-actions he believes the men have to his method of supervising. Depending on Bruce's response, Cole will know what to do and say.

THE ESSENCE OF THIS APPROACH

Cole gives Bruce the opportunity to rectify the matter without the need for disciplinary embarrassment.

B. Cole can tell Bruce what he has discovered and heard, point out to Bruce what there is about his manner and bearing that alarms or upsets the men, and urge him to correct the impression.

THE ESSENCE OF THIS APPROACH

Cole presents the problem directly to Bruce, but still gives him a chance to correct his stance without excessive embarrassment to him.

C. Cole can call in all of his foreman and say:

- From time to time I have noticed one or two of you creating an impression among your men which I am sure you don't intend to convey.
- I'd rather not pinpoint which ones are involved, since any one of you might inadvertently do the same thing once in a while.
- Let's review the matter for future avoidance and present correction, as applicable.
- When you walk around supervising you should appear casual, as though your being there is the most natural thing in the world.
- Above all, avoid being or appearing officious, snoopy or frightening.

THE ESSENCE OF THIS APPROACH

Cole avoids embarrassing Bruce at the same time that he repeats a general lesson in effective supervision: the proper demeanor required while supervising.

ADAPTING THESE SOLUTIONS TO YOUR OWN WORK

Your assistants must, of course, be constantly supervising their men. This requires that they move about among them all the time and find out what's going on.

While doing this, however, they must adopt and demonstrate a casual and natural air, so that the men won't resent or fear their approach or presence.

This attitude toward how best to supervise is not necessarily something that a supervisor acquires all by himself. Make sure that all of your assistants understand the need for this technique, know how to apply it and actually do.

SITUATION NUMBER 67 — The manager who supervises inadequately or improperly by getting involved in work he's supposed to be supervising.

INCIDENT

Hall Madden is maintenance foreman. He reports to Ian Nathans.

On his usual rounds Ian has frequently noticed that Hall is himself doing repairs on a piece of equipment while his men stand around and do nothing, watching him. Meanwhile other men not involved with that particular piece of equipment are less productive than they can and should be, either because they are waiting for specific instructions from Hall or because he isn't around to urge them on.

ALTERNATE SOLUTIONS

A. Ian can simply tell Hall that:

- His job is to supervise, not to do.
- In an emergency, where he is convinced that he must himself do a repair, he is first to call Ian so that *he* can replace Hall temporarily as supervisor.
- The reason for all of this is that while Hall might be saving the company money by doing the repair himself on one piece of equipment, he is costing the company a

greater amount of money by the lowered productivity of the other men.

THE ESSENCE OF THIS APPROACH

Ian lays it on the line on what he wants Hall to do, at the same time that he explains why he wants it done that way.

B. Ian can call Hall in and say:

- I've observed you doing repairs yourself while your other men are less productive than they'd be if you supervised.
- Why do you do those repairs yourself?
- Are you aware of the lessened productivity when you aren't supervising properly and of how much this is costing the company?
- What do you suggest we do about this?

THE ESSENCE OF THIS APPROACH

Ian presents Hall the problem as Ian sees it, asking Hall how *he* sees it. This places the burden squarely on Hall to recognize the consequences of what he is doing and come up with an acceptable solution.

C. When Ian sees Hall so engaged, he can immediately assume the role of first-line supervisor (without saying anything or acting in any way to embarrass or demean Hall) for as long as Hall is so engaged. Then, when Hall has finished what he's working on, Ian can tell him what he's done and why.

THE ESSENCE OF THIS APPROACH

Ian brings the matter sharply to Hall's attention in the hope that he'll get the message that he has inconvenienced Ian by not doing his own job properly.

ADAPTING THESE SOLUTIONS TO YOUR OWN WORK

A first-line supervisor must be a *supervisor* and not a *doer.* Any activity which he is supposed to delegate *must* be delegated.

When a supervisor is doing what an hourly employee should be doing, that supervisor is making it likely that the other hourly employees will be less productive because they are not being properly supervised.

You must make this clear to your supervisory assistants and tell them that if they must at any time *not* supervise, they should let you know so you can provide the proper supervision during that time.

SITUATION NUMBER 68 — The manager who supervises his assistants inadequately or improperly by criticizing them while others can hear.

INCIDENT

Lionel O'Farrell supervises fifteen clerks. He works for Marcus Palmer.

On occasion Marcus has heard Lionel criticizing one or another of his clerks, in most cases for mistakes that merited attention, in such a way that other clerks also working under Lionel can hear what Lionel is saying.

ALTERNATE SOLUTIONS

A. Marcus can call Lionel in and ask him:

* Are you aware that you have criticized some of your clerks within the hearing of others?
* Do you know the effect this has on both that clerk and the others?
* Won't you please make a strong effort not to do this again?

Marcus can then check up to see whether Lionel is adhering to his promise to avoid that pitfall.

THE ESSENCE OF THIS APPROACH

Marcus brings the problem to Lionel's attention, gives him an opportunity to become aware of his wrongdoing and gives him every opportunity to correct it by himself.

B. Marcus can say to Lionel:

- I've noticed you criticizing (Marcus mentions the names of the specific clerks) in the presence of others (Marcus names them too).
- This is bad management practice because (Marcus tells him why).
- Please avoid doing this again.
- I shall be checking up on this again.

THE ESSENCE OF THIS APPROACH

Marcus names the actual people involved in the situations in question, thus removing any possible doubt of the poor practice in which Lionel is engaging. Marcus then tells Lionel why the practice is wrong and strongly urges him to avoid it in future.

ADAPTING THESE SOLUTIONS TO YOUR OWN WORK

The only time that a supervisor is justified in criticizing one of his assistants in the hearing or presence of another is when that assistant has openly defied the supervisor in the presence or hearing of the other. Even then, the public reproval must be limited to preventing the others from falsely thinking that anyone can defy the supervisor and get away with it.

In all other cases the supervisor must clearly understand, accept and implement the principles that:

- Criticizing an assistant is a private matter between the critic and the assistant.
- Failure to observe this truth results not only in the demoralization of the one criticized but also in the embarrassment of the one who hears or sees it and shouldn't.
- The other assistants will also realize that they, too, might be subjected to the same treatment and might therefore try to cover up any mistakes which could warrant criticism.

13

How to Handle
The Poorly Motivated Assistant

In the following situations note that the concept of
motivation is here treated as a combination of management knowledge, abilities, attitudes and habits. Before you try to motivate an assistant who needs it, you
must first make sure that he is capable of doing well
in a job for which he has enough knowledge, experience
and the proper conditions. Only then can motivation —
in the true sense — be attempted with a reasonable
chance for success.

SITUATION NUMBER 69 — The poorly motivated assistant
who feels he has too many responsibilities.

INCIDENT

Mason Raleigh is office manager. His boss is Mervin St.
John.

Lately, Mervin has been noticing a deterioration in the
quantity and quality of the various office functions under Mason's authority. Mervin knows that Mason is a very knowledgeable, capable and experienced office manager and that the
conditions under which Mason and his people work are entirely
satisfactory. Mervin brings his observations to Mason's attention
and asks him why the activities have deteriorated.

Mason replies that he cannot possibly supervise all of the departments and people under him as effectively as he could if he had fewer responsibilities. He intimates that he has become discouraged by the increase in his duties as a result of company growth and that this has tended to diminish his normal supervisory drive.

ALTERNATE SOLUTIONS

A. Mervin can reduce Mason's duties to the extent necessary and tell him that now there is no reason why he cannot return to his previous degree of motivation and good results. Mervin must, of course, indicate that now there can be no excuse for any but the highest drive and outcome.

THE ESSENCE OF THIS APPROACH

Mervin eliminates the cause of Mason's lessened motivation and indicates firmly that there is now no reason why Mason shouldn't be entirely satisfied with his work load.

B. Mervin can investigate Mason's work load and find out how accurate the latter's assessment of the burdensomeness of his duties is. If he discovers that there is no real substance to Mason's complaint, he must then try to find out what Mason's real problem is, and then address himself to it.

THE ESSENCE OF THIS APPROACH

Mervin doesn't take it for granted that just because Mason says his workload is too heavy, Mason is necessarily accurate in his assessment. Mervin finds out for himself and acts accordingly.

ADAPTING THESE SOLUTIONS TO YOUR OWN WORK

When an assistant says that he isn't doing his best because an excessive workload is discouraging him, your best bet is to tell him that you're sorry to hear that and that you want to think about how best to help him; then, without letting on that you might be questioning the validity of his complaint, personally investigate the situation. If his workload *is* excessive, relieve him of the excess. If it isn't, find out what's really bothering him and address yourself to that.

SITUATION NUMBER 70 — The poorly motivated assistant who doesn't like the work he's assigned.

INCIDENT

Myron Tarr is a production foreman under Neal Valdes. Neal has repeatedly told Myron that housekeeping is an important part of a foreman's duties, but Myron doesn't care for that responsibility and pays little attention to it. Despite Myron's attitude toward housekeeping, he is a very conscientious and effective foreman in every other respect.

ALTERNATE SOLUTIONS

A. Neal can tell Myron that he simply must pay the proper attention to housekeeping no matter what his attitude is about it, simply because:

- Neal insists on it and is Myron's boss, and
- Regardless of whether Myron agrees, Neal *knows* how important good housekeeping is to profitable management in a production area.

Neal adds that Myron's continued failure to pay the proper attention to housekeeping will result in an unsatisfactory rating for that portion of Neal's evaluation of Myron's results.

THE ESSENCE OF THIS APPROACH

Neal realizes that he probably won't be able to motivate Myron *positively* and adopts his only alternative — *negative* motivation.

B. Neal can try again to motivate Myron by telling him:

- Good housekeeping leads to more profitable production.
- It also raises morale.
- It makes a better impression on visitors.
- Please consider all of this as important as the other things you already do, which you do well.

THE ESSENCE OF THIS APPROACH

Neal appeals to Myron's generally good attitude toward his job and tries to get Myron to *want* to feel that housekeeping is important.

C. Neal can make a survey of time wasted and production diminished as a result of specific examples of poor housekeeping. He can then present the facts to Myron and deal with him in the same way as he would with any other foreman's duty

THE ESSENCE OF THIS APPROACH

Neal treats Myron's one shortcoming as a *production* failure, something which Myron will readily understand and be willing to remedy.

ADAPTING THESE SOLUTIONS TO YOUR OWN WORK

Many management employees have preferences and dislikes regarding the work they are supposed to do. Consciously or unconsciously, they will pay sufficient attention to those activities they enjoy and tend to play down or disregard those they don't enjoy.

This really amounts to motivation. When you have such a poorly motivated assistant, tackle the motivational aspects first and relate them to the specific activity which is being neglected.

SITUATION NUMBER 71 — The poorly motivated assistant who feels he doesn't get enough recognition.

INCIDENT

Wes Adelson is one of several production superintendents in the company working under Norton Wright.

Wes has complained to Norton frequently that he, Wes, was getting consistently better results than the other superintendents, but that they weren't acknowledged as such. As a matter of fact, Wes is convinced that the others are favored because they've been working for the company longer.

His major objection is to the praise that is constantly heaped on their heads, in contrast to the very little recognition he thinks he gets for his excellent performance.

Norton admits to himself that Wes' results are generally far superior to those of the others.

ALTERNATE SOLUTIONS

A. Norton can call Wes in and speak to him along these lines:

- You and I know that your work is superior to that of the others.
- We don't really mean to exalt them and belittle you. It's just that there is a tendency to give greater recognition to the men who've been around for a long time.
- I'll continue to recommend you for monetary increases wherever possible.
- Forget about this matter of who gets greater recognition and derive your satisfaction from our joint knowledge of the great contribution you're making.

THE ESSENCE OF THIS APPROACH

Norton tries to get Wes to substitute real recognition of his merits for the public recognition he seems to want, thus avoiding a problem that Norton might otherwise have with the other superintendents.

B. Norton can increase the number of occasions when he gives public recognition to Wes for his deserved results, without in any way diminishing the recognition that the others seem to require. He must, however, make sure not to praise anyone for something he doesn't deserve to be praised for.

The clue lies in finding something good to say about each superintendent who merits it, making sure to give greater recognition to greater merit where it occurs.

THE ESSENCE OF THIS APPROACH

Norton is fair to Wes without hurting the other superintendents.

ADAPTING THESE SOLUTIONS TO YOUR OWN WORK

It's a natural and normal tendency for employees to want to be acknowledged, recognized and praised for their excellence. They will also want this to be public as well as private. Such praise must be sparing and always merited. If one employee or more do only adequate work, they may still want recognition for that. If they don't realize that their work is only minimally acceptable, you will have to try to accomplish *both* of these objectives simultaneously:

- Stimulate and motivate them to do better, if possible.
- Praise or recognize them for anything they do that merits it.

SITUATION NUMBER 72 — The poorly motivated assistant who lacks ambition.

INCIDENT

Pat Baker had been a competent, high-level clerical employee for fifteen years. A vacancy opened up in the office for a supervisor over clerical employees not in Pat's section.

The office manager, Rudy Wallace, asked Pat's boss whether he thought Pat would fill the vacancy well, would be willing to take the job and could easily be replaced in his current tasks. Pat's boss replied in the affirmative to all of the questions.

Rudy then approached Pat and said:

- A vacancy has occurred in the next section of the office for a supervisor of clerical employees.
- Your boss has recommended you for the job.
- If you take it we'll give you all the necessary training.
- Are you interested?

Pat replied that he wasn't entirely sure that he wanted the job because he was enjoying what he was now doing, but that he would be willing to give it a try if both Rudy and Pat's boss wanted him to.

After the needed training Pat was officially installed in the job.

When three months had elapsed Rudy was convinced, despite all of his efforts to motivate Pat to try harder, that Pat regretted his decision and really didn't want to be a supervisor. Rudy was convinced, further, that Pat's major problem with respect to his new job was that he lacked ambition for advancement with the company and would really prefer to be back in his own, old job.

ALTERNATE SOLUTIONS

A. Rudy can call Pat in and speak to him this way:

- As you know from what I've been calling to your attention during the last few weeks, your work as a supervisor isn't as good as was your work as a clerk.
- I still feel that you have the ability to become a truly effective supervisor and would like to see that happen.
- But that will come about only if you really want to do what you have to do, with my help, to reach that objective.
- I'd like you to tell me now, once and for all, whether you want to make that effort.

If Rudy gets the feeling that Pat will make the effort, he can express his satisfaction at that decision and arrange for the necessary steps to help Pat make and keep the grade.

THE ESSENCE OF THIS APPROACH

Rudy takes the last step required before coming to a decision on the matter, and gives Pat his last chance to say yea or nay about his ambition.

B. Rudy can come to the conclusion, either after he's given Alternate Solution A. a chance or without even using it, that Pat simply has no ambition for the new job. He then calls Pat in and says:

- When I first asked you whether you wanted to be a supervisor you weren't particularly enthusiastic about it, but we both felt that we ought to give you a chance at it.
- Unfortunately you haven't done well as a supervisor, despite all my efforts to remotivate and help you.

- I must therefore take you away from your present job — in the company's interest — and put someone else in that place.
- Since you've been a long-time and loyal employee, and have much to contribute to the company in your previous type of work, I'm going to assume that you'd like to be relieved of supervisory responsibilities and put back into your previous kind of work.
- I can't return you to your old job because that would represent a demotion; that is against our policy and against good management practice.
- Therefore, I'm going to announce that there is a need for your services in a newly created job — special assistant to me — and continue to pay you your present salary.
- I want you, however, to remember this: If your work isn't up to my expectations (despite all my efforts to help you) you'll be separated from the company. Also, since you demonstrated — by your failure to do a good supervisory job — that you lack company ambition, you will never be eligible for any further advancement, and you'll receive no increases in salary until the salary for your old job exceeds the salary you are now getting.

THE ESSENCE OF THIS APPROACH

Rudy faces apparent reality, gives Pat one last chance to quit if he wants to, saves Pat's face, avoids a bad management practice, utilizes the best Pat has to offer and makes clear to Pat that he has selected his niche for the rest of his time with the company — although he still must perform satisfactorily in his new job.

ADAPTING THESE SOLUTIONS TO YOUR OWN JOB

It's preferable not to appoint a non-management employee to a management position, no matter what other qualifications he may have, if he lacks the kind of ambition necessary for that jump.

If, however, you've gambled and lost, you really have only two alternatives:

- Put him into a non-management position where he can make a valuable contribution, without any inferences or implications that he has been demoted.
- Separate him because you can't demote him and he isn't worth saving through the device described just above.

SITUATION NUMBER 73 — The poorly motivated assistant, some of whose own assistants earn more than he does.

INCIDENT

Sheldon Walker is a production foreman. His company has a policy that when the hourly employees work overtime, the appropriate foreman stays with them. Since the men are given overtime pay and the foremen are not paid hourly, the foremen's salary and other privileges (like not being docked for certain hours not worked) are — along with the right to be a part of management — adequate compensation for working overtime hours without extra pay.

The foremen agree with this management policy, but complain to the superintendent, Virgil Calvert, that:

- Many of their men, because of their overtime pay, wind up with a higher annual wage than their salaries.
- This adversely affects their authoritativeness over the men.

Virgil investigates this situation and finds that the foremen's assertions are true.

ALTERNATE SOLUTIONS

A. Virgil can ask the President to institute and announce a remuneration system for the production department which works somewhat like this:

- Every foreman's results are analyzed annually for their contribution to profit.
- Any one foreman whose results make an unusual contribution to profit will receive a sufficient amount of

additional money representing his just share in the resulting profits.

THE ESSENCE OF THIS APPROACH

Deserving foremen will earn more money than their base salaries, said amount having to be higher than what their men total.

B. Virgil can ask his president to authorize a policy along these lines (and so publicized):

- At the end of the year the total earnings for any man under any one foreman will be compared to that foreman's gross salary for that year.
- Any foreman whose salary is less than that of any of his men or only equal to it will be given, early in the following year, an additional amount of money.
- This is not to be thought of as a bonus; it's an effort to assure that foremen earn more (by at least $1000) than any of their men, regardless of the fact that the men are paid extra for their overtime work when the foremen (who work right alongside of them) do not.

THE ESSENCE OF THIS APPROACH

The foremen do get paid more than their men and the men will recognize this fact.

ADAPTING THESE SOLUTIONS TO YOUR OWN WORK

No matter how much one might want to disbelieve it, men do tend to respect their foremen less if the latter earn less than they do.

A foreman must *not* be given overtime pay because he must think of his job as unlimited in hours. If his men work overtime, so must he. But he must *not* be rewarded for this on an hourly basis.

The assumption must be made that his working alongside of them during overtime hours represents a contribution to profit which deserves a reward which, incidentally, also solves the problem of the discrepancies in earnings.

14

How to Handle The Assistant Who Hurts the Company

In the following situations note that there is a certain sequence which should be followed: First you must become aware that an assistant may be hurting the company. Next you must investigate to check the accuracy and validity of your awareness. Then you must find out whether the assistant is aware of both what he is doing and the fact that it is hurting the company. Only then are you in a position to judge whether his acts are remediable or not, and can proceed accordingly.

SITUATION NUMBER 74 — The assistant who hurts the company by criticizing it in his community.

INCIDENT

Elliot Daniels was a first-line supervisor in his company's office complex, working for Greg Vale.

Elliot was very active — and popular — in his community, especially in the Rotary Club, which met every week (on a Tuesday) from noon to 1:00 P.M., at a location fifteen minutes drive from the company.

When the company acquired a new Chief Executive Officer,

determined to convert the company from a losing enterprise into a profitable business, many changes began to take place. The results were almost unbelievable, especially in the area of increased productivity by all concerned — at less cost than previously.

One of the new rules was that salaried employees (management as well as non-management) could not have more than half an hour for lunch, and were free to eat it in the company cafeteria or anywhere else they liked (except at their or someone else's desk) as long as no more than thirty minutes elapsed between their official lunchtime beginning and the moment that they were back at their desks doing their work.

Elliot told his fellow Rotarians (many of whom were leading citizens dealing with the company in one way or another) — as well as other people in the community — that:

- The company had become inhumane.
- The new administration was inconsiderate and unfair.
- That he couldn't attend Rotary meetings because of the new policy.
- That company morale had deteriorated considerably.

Word of Elliot's pronouncements repeatedly came to Greg's attention.

ALTERNATE SOLUTIONS

A. Greg calls Elliot in and speaks to him as follows:

- It has come to my attention that you are complaining in the community about one of our policies.
- It doesn't make any difference which policy we're talking about.
- Is it true that you are doing this?

If Elliot denies the allegation, Greg expresses himself as pleased that that is so.

THE ESSENCE OF THIS APPROACH

Greg gives Elliot a chance to defend himself, save face, or avoid any wrongdoing in which he may be engaging.

B. Greg can investigate the validity of the rumors and if he finds that Elliott *is* voicing his complaints in the community, can speak to him along these lines:

- I had heard that you were complaining in the community about our new policy regarding lunch.
- I investigated carefully and discovered that you have been doing this at least to the following . . .
- I'm disappointed in you because you are otherwise a very valuable assistant to me.
- Good management absolutely requires that when you have a complaint about *anything* in the company you come to me.
- As long as you work for this company you absolutely must *not* complain in your community about *anything* that goes on in this company.
- I shall expect you not to do that sort of thing again.

THE ESSENCE OF THIS APPROACH

Greg first arms himself with the facts. He then tells Elliot where he erred and why, and that he mustn't do it again.

C. Greg can call Elliot in and say:

- I've heard that you've been complaining in the community about our new lunch policy.
- It doesn't matter too much whether you actually did it or not, because people are saying that you did.
- You have to be extremely careful not to give that impression.
- The best way to do so is to come to me with any gripes that you have and not say anything to anyone else about them.

THE ESSENCE OF THIS APPROACH

Greg whittles the issue down to the effect on both Elliot and the company of even being thought of as complaining outside of the organization about the company. Greg suggests to Elliot a way of avoiding repetitions of that situation.

ADAPTING THESE SOLUTIONS TO YOUR OWN WORK

Perhaps you should add, to the many items about which you orient your assistants, a caution about talking about the company outside of official channels.

Tell them exactly what you mean by this, why this is important not only to the company but to them — a griper demeans himself — and encourage them to come to you with their complaints.

If you discover that one of your assistants is violating your rule, treat such violation as a breach of his management responsibilities.

SITUATION NUMBER 75 — The assistant who hurts the company by behavior in public places where he is known as a company employee.

INCIDENT

Hank Edison is a foreman in Morris Tate's department.

A number of the company's customers whose business establishments are in the community where the company is located have complained to the company's sales manager that Hank — who frequents their business places — is noisy and quarrelsome. He does this even when there are other patrons in the store or other place.

Some of the patrons know that Hank works at the plant which supplies some of the goods they buy from that company, and have told the owners that they might have to avoid coming in in the evening or weekends when Hank is there. The sales manager has reported this to Morris and asked him to help.

At work, Hank is conscientious and effective. He displays none of the traits there that he's described as manifesting away from his job.

ALTERNATE SOLUTIONS

A. Morris can call Hank in and say:

- You know that I consider you one of my best foremen.
- I am told that you are considered noisy and quarrelsome

by some of the owners of establishments which you frequent on the outside.

- Essentially, that's none of my business, except that many
  of the people who complain about this are our customers
  and they know that you work for us.
- They say that their patrons are avoiding coming in when
  you're there and that this hurts their business.
- Our sales manager is afraid that this might hurt his ability
  to continue selling them our products.
- Whether their accusations are true or not, I'm sure I
  can rely on you to avoid giving anyone a false impression
  of you *or* the company.

THE ESSENCE OF THIS APPROACH

Morris appeals to Hank's general loyalty to the company by
asking him to avoid embarrassing it on the outside.

B. Morris can call what appears to be a regular foreman's
meeting at which he covers a number of important matters; then,
as part of the agenda, Morris says:

- As you know, I periodically talk to you about the importance to our company of matters not directly related to
  your foremanship responsibilities.
- This afternoon I'd like to select another topic of importance to all of us.
- One of the objectives of our company is to maintain the
  proper image in our community, both for its own sake and
  because of its impact on sales.
- You are the management representatives of the company
  wherever you go, and are known and considered as such.
- How you conduct yourselves on the outside reflects on
  you *and* the company.
- As long as you maintain the right image we both benefit,
  because your personal security and prosperity depend
  on that of the company.
- Anyone who acts in an undignified or indecent manner
  on the outside hurts not only himself but also all of you
  and the company.

- I know that all of you will want always to bear this in mind and act accordingly.

THE ESSENCE OF THIS APPROACH

Morris doesn't accuse or embarrass anyone unless the shoe fits. He gets his point across correctively and subtly to the one who provoked it and possibly helps to prevent anyone else from going astray.

ADAPTING THESE SOLUTIONS TO YOUR OWN WORK

Your assistants owe it to themselves, their company and you to create and maintain a desirable image in their respective communities.

The rationale is that they are part of your management and are known to be such in the places they frequent.

They must be impressed with the importance of the proper image, and they must be warned to desist from known cases of acting otherwise. While what they do on the outside is basically their own business, it becomes yours if that behavior threatens your company's reputation or prosperity.

SITUATION NUMBER 76 — The assistant who hurts the company by urging other assistants to be less productive.

INCIDENT

Hirsch Falter is foreman over one production assembly operation. He receives the components on which his men must work from Manfred Saltz, another foreman. Both report to Ira Farber.

In his periodic checking on productivity Ira finds that the productivity in both departments is below his established and communicated schedules. He asks Hirsch why *his* productivity is low and Hirsch replies that he is keeping up with Manfred's flow. Ira then asks Manfred about *his* flow and he replies that he is keeping up with Hirsch's ability to process what Manfred can yield.

While Manfred is reluctant to say so, Ira gets the distinct

impression that Hirsch has asked Manfred to slow down and Manfred has done so.

ALTERNATE SOLUTIONS

A. Ira can speak to Hirsch as follows:

- Your productivity is lower than schedule.
- Investigation reveals that Manfred can supply a greater flow than you can keep up with.
- Let's see why you're falling below schedule and what we can do about it.

THE ESSENCE OF THIS APPROACH

Ira avoids a confrontation on the collusion issue and takes steps to prevent its recurrence while concentrating on the main objective: meeting schedules.

B. Ira can confront Hirsch with what he infers about the request to Manfred to slow down and check on the accuracy of the inference. If Ira is convinced that Hirsch has done just that, Ira can reprove Hirsch and warn him against repeating the wrong practice.

Ira can then repeat the process with Manfred, only this time it would revolve around his responding to an improper request.

THE ESSENCE OF THIS APPROACH

Ira faces right up to the undesirable management practice, giving each man, separately, the chance to justify himself.

C. Ira can call both Hirsch and Manfred in for a meeting and address them thus:

- Each of you is falling below schedule.
- Let's see why, right now.
- Here's what we're going to do about solving that problem.

THE ESSENCE OF THIS APPROACH

Ira confronts *both* foremen with the basic problem simultaneously and seeks a mutual solution without raising the question of the collusion.

ADAPTING THESE SOLUTIONS TO YOUR OWN WORK

You must always establish and communicate to all of your assistants your minimally acceptable schedules for the productivity flow in which they are all involved. You're better off if each one of them knows not only his own schedule but the total schedule.

You must then carefully check this schedule quite frequently. When you discover that one or more of the foremen isn't meeting schedule, find out why. If one of the reasons is collusion, deal with this as a separate issue while you get the flow back on schedule at the same time.

SITUATION NUMBER 77 — The assistant who hurts the company by incurring excessive indebtedness in his personal affairs.

INCIDENT

Jeff Gamby is an office supervisor working for Len Ramos.

In the last few months the company has been contacted by a number of outside entities in a number of ways regarding Jeff's personal indebtedness: credit bureaus, garnishments, debtors, etc.

Len has called Jeff in to ask him why this has been happening. Jeff says that he's been having a number of personal financial problems which have caused him to borrow heavily without being able to pay back when he should have.

ALTERNATE SOLUTIONS

A. Len can tell Jeff that:

- He sympathizes with Jeff's problems.
- He cannot have company time taken up with responses to outside agencies related to Jeff's personal indebtedness.
- Jeff's personal status regarding credit could have an adverse effect on the company's standing in the financial community.
- Jeff will simply have to find some way of solving his problems without involving the company.

- If Jeff cannot do this the company may have to separate him.

THE ESSENCE OF THIS APPROACH

Len puts Jeff on notice that he mustn't hurt the company with his personal debt problems and that he simply must prevent a recurrence.

B. Len can call Jeff in and ask him what the problem is. If Jeff can assure him that it will not happen again, Len can tell him that he's glad that that's so and that it cannot really be permitted to happen again.

On the other hand, if Len isn't satisfied that it *will* be solved the right way, he can suggest to Jeff that he sit down with the company personnel manager to discuss the whole situation and see what can be done to clear the matter up.

Len then follows up on that conversation and takes the necessary steps to assure that Jeff will not again hurt the company by his personal indebtedness.

THE ESSENCE OF THIS APPROACH

Len offers Jeff proper company help to solve his personal problems, at the same time that he makes sure that they are either solved or no longer affect the company.

ADAPTING THESE SOLUTIONS TO YOUR OWN WORK

If any of your assistants are in a personal financial situation which involves the company you must take all necessary steps to prevent a continuation and/or recurrence of this problem.

If your company's personnel department is equipped to help such an assistant, that help should be offered, but under no circumstances can the problem be permitted to persist or recur.

SITUATION NUMBER 78 — The assistant who hurts the company by discussing unpleasant aspects of his home life among his fellow workers.

INCIDENT

Jess Hammill is one of five supervisors reporting to Lee Paly. On a number of occasions one or another of the other supervisors has come to Lee to complain that:

- When they are at lunch with Jess he tends to dominate the conversation with talk about his home life.
- All of his statements deal with how unpleasant it is for him at home.
- The others are not only bored but also embarrassed by Jess' tirades.
- They'd like Lee to arrange for them not to have to take their lunch in the same place or at the same time as Jess.

Jess is, in every other respect, a loyal and effective supervisor.

ALTERNATE SOLUTIONS

A. Lee can so arrange Jess' working time that he has to eat lunch alone. If Jess objects to the arrangement, Lee can tell him why it was set up that way.

Jess could then take the initiative to assure Lee that if he's put back on the old schedule he won't continue the undesired practice.

THE ESSENCE OF THIS APPROACH

Lee avoids the problem and its concomitant embarrassment.

B. Lee can call Jess in and tell him:

- That Lee considers him an entirely satisfactory supervisor.
- What the other supervisors have said.
- That it's up to Jess to settle the problem because Jess' behavior is hurting the others' morale, and this cannot be tolerated.

THE ESSENCE OF THIS APPROACH

Lee gets right to the heart of the matter with Jess, pointing out that the latter mustn't let his otherwise excellent record be spoiled by a habit which can easily be changed.

ADAPTING THESE SOLUTIONS TO YOUR OWN WORK

The morale of *all* of your assistants is as important as that of any one of them; therefore, if any one of them is hurting *their* morale, you must do what you can to stop the relevant acts.

The others have a right to engage in pleasant conversation during their lunch periods. Anyone who interferes with this should be given a chance to desist and, if he doesn't, should be isolated.

If even that doesn't work, then you have to ask yourself which is the greater good for the company: the professional contribution of the pest or the adverse effect on the professional contributions of those pestered.

SITUATION NUMBER 79 — The assistant who hurts the company by setting a bad example of work habits for his assistants.

INCIDENT

Joel Insull is office manager and has four supervisors under him. His boss is Kermit O'Hara.

On his regular rounds of inspection in Joel's bailiwick, Kermit notices that the supervisors in general, have sloppy desks with papers lying all over with no apparent order. He also infers that this is contributing to a waste of time when they have to look for specific papers and/or use their desk tops for paperwork.

Kermit has come to the same conclusion about Joel's own desk and efficiency.

ALTERNATE SOLUTIONS

A. Kermit can bring to Joel's attention the disorder that characterizes his desk and go on to say that:

- Kermit is convinced that this has got to affect adversely Joel's paperwork efficiency.
- Joel's assistants have the same kind of desk-top confusion, with the same resulting inefficiency.
- Joel must change his own work habits in the proper way and then see to it that his men do the same.

THE ESSENCE OF THIS APPROACH

Kermit points out to Joel exactly what he thinks Joel is doing wrong, emphasizes the undesirable effect of his bad example and asks him to set the matter right.

B. Kermit can ask Joel to accompany him on a tour, first, of the assistants' offices and then of his — Joel's — own, without making any comments to Joel about his — Kermit's — conclusions.

Kermit then asks Joel to tell him what he's discovered. If the answer is not adequate for Kermit's purposes, he *tells* Joel what the assessment should have been.

In either case, Kermit then asks Joel to straighten out the situation.

THE ESSENCE OF THIS APPROACH

Kermit gives Joel an opportunity to come to his own conclusions about what's bothering Kermit, and then sees to it that Joel acts properly.

C. Kermit can arrange for a brief course in the proper and orderly care of paper in an office and have both Joel and *all* of his assistants attend simultaneously.

The course can stress the following points:

- Some of them have desks which defy proper orderliness.
- This adversely affects efficiency.
- Here are some basic principles of proper desk-top arrangement.
- All present are expected to change their habits in that regard.

THE ESSENCE OF THIS APPROACH

Kermit gets his message across about paperwork at the same time as he gives Joel a chance to recognize that he has been presenting a bad example and had better stop doing that.

ADAPTING THESE SOLUTIONS TO YOUR OWN WORK

Whatever practices are desirable for a man's assistants — whether or not *he* recognizes them as desirable — must be part of his own work habits. To begin with, his own habits are bound to serve as an example for his men. If these habits are bad, he has very little chance of correcting those of his men unless he sets a good example himself.

15

How to Handle
The Disloyal Assistant

In the following situations note that loyalty is emphasized as an integral part of an assistant's duty to his company and his boss. Notice that where a manager feels that one or more of his assistants are disloyal, he must first make them realize that they are and ascertain how such realization affects them. If they don't care about that kind of attitude and can't be made to consider it important, you have to make up your mind whether you can continue to have such assistants under you.

SITUATION NUMBER 80 — The disloyal assistant who is constantly complaining about facets of his work.

INCIDENT

Jonas Lamont is head of a group of salaried employees. His boss is Josh Kane.

In a reorganization of the office Jonas has had taken away from him about half of his assistants, who were assigned elsewhere. Jonas' duties have also been expanded to include certain non-delegable tasks.

Jonas has repeatedly complained to Josh that he feels demeaned by the change, but Josh has as often explained that it was no reflection on him as an individual. The change was simply necessary for company profit.

Nevertheless, Jonas keeps on complaining to anyone who'll listen, including his own assistants, saying that Josh has been unfair to him. In addition, Jonas' work has deteriorated.

ALTERNATE SOLUTIONS

A. Josh can call Jonas in and:

• Tell him that he has heard Jonas' complaints too often himself, has heard that Jonas is complaining to anyone and everyone and is disappointed that Jonas' work is inferior.

• Try to persuade Jonas to change his ways.

• Warn him that if he doesn't, Josh will be forced to request Jonas' separation.

THE ESSENCE OF THIS APPROACH

Josh makes one last effort to remove the problem, at the same time that he makes it plain that it *is* the last chance that Josh has.

B. Josh can ask Jonas:

• Do you see what you are doing as being consistent with the loyalty you owe me?

• How important to you is that loyalty?

• Let's re-examine the problem about which you've been complaining.

• This is as far as I can go in solving the problem: . . .

• How far can you go in adjusting yourself to your new duties?

• Will you promise me that from now on you'll complain only to me?

THE ESSENCE OF THIS APPROACH

Josh puts the subject of loyalty squarely before Jonas and makes that the major issue. At the same time, he tries to satisfy Jonas regarding his job.

ADAPTING THESE SOLUTIONS TO YOUR OWN WORK

Complaints by your assistants should be encouraged as long as they are made only to you. You should point out to them that you are always ready to listen and try to help them.

You should also make it plain, however, that complaints about their jobs, you or the company made to anyone other than you are marks of disloyalty to you, and that loyalty is one of their most important duties. They always have the right to appeal your decisions and acts as long as they tell you first that that's what they want to do.

SITUATION NUMBER 81 — The disloyal assistant who is always talking about looking for a better job.

INCIDENT

Anselm Baldwin is a supervisor working for Zach Cameron.

Lately Zach has been hearing that Anselm is saying, to both his fellow supervisors and his own assistants, that he isn't satisfied with his present job in the company. He is also heard to say that he doesn't think he has any chance for advancement there and is looking around for a better job in another company.

Anselm has told this to Zach also.

ALTERNATE SOLUTIONS

A. Zach can call Anselm in and ask him:

- Is it true that you're not satisfied with your job?
- If it isn't, then why am I hearing that you aren't? If it is, why don't we try to straighten this out once and for all?

Then, depending on Anselm's replies, Zach can either:

- Urge him to stop talking loosely, or
- Arrive at a method for getting Anselm to be satisfied with his job, or
- Tell him that he's free to start looking (while Zach does the same without saying so).

THE ESSENCE OF THIS APPROACH

Zach tries to arrive at the true state of affairs regarding Anselm's loyalty and satisfaction with the job; then Zach acts in a straightforward manner to solve the problem, whatever it is.

B. Zach can tell Anselm that regardless of whether he's satisfied with his job he must display the proper loyalty to Zach. Part of this consists of not going about talking as he has been doing. If Anselm wants to quit, that's fine; but as long as he works for Zach he must be loyal to him.

THE ESSENCE OF THIS APPROACH

Zach places the emphasis on the loyalty and makes it clear that that duty is as important as any other which Anselm has.

C. Zach can assume that Anselm is a disgruntled employee who will never again be satisfied, if he ever was, with the job he has. This kind of man is certainly not good material for promotion.

Zach says nothing to Anselm but starts to look for his replacement. When he finds it he gives Anselm notice and then separates him.

THE ESSENCE OF THIS APPROACH

Zach wastes no more time on an assistant who has clearly demonstrated that his disloyalty is a symptom of his basic uselessness, since he started griping, to the company.

ADAPTING THESE SOLUTIONS TO YOUR OWN WORK

When an assistant starts talking to others about looking for another job you have two choices:

If he's valuable to you, give him another chance to stop

griping publicly and try to adjust to his job for satisfaction. If, however, he's not particularly valuable to you, you're better off taking it for granted that he'll be no great asset to you and the sooner you replace him the better for all concerned.

SITUATION NUMBER 82 — The disloyal assistant who uses drugs in his personal life.

INCIDENT

Claude Danziger is a supervisor who works under Vaughn Zimmer. One of Claude's fellow-supervisors comes to Vaughn and says:

- I don't want to be a squealer, but I value this company and don't want any harm to come to it.
- I live next door to Claude and have seen and heard what goes on at some of the parties he gives.
- I have reason to believe that he and some of his guests smoke marijuana at those parties.
- I've asked him about it and he denies it, but I'm quite sure I'm right.
- I asked him either to stop it or be more discreet because he is known in the community as an employee here and might cast discredit on the company if he were caught.
- I told him that if he didn't take care I'd tell you about it, and why.

Vaughn thanks the supervisor, tells him to say nothing to anybody and goes to find Claude. Vaughn tells him what he has heard, refuses to implicate the other supervisor and goes on to say:

- What you do in your personal life is, of course, your own business, but if it adversely affects the company it's *my* business.
- I'm not interested in whether what I've heard is true or not, but I'm asking you to prevent anything like this from attracting unfavorable attention to us.
- Also, if you *are* doing what I've heard, it's bad for you as well as for the company.

- I consider that you owe it to the company and me, as a matter of loyalty, not to let anything like that take place.

Some time later Vaughn hears from a number of company employees, each separately, the same story that the supervisor had first told him.

ALTERNATE SOLUTIONS

A. Vaughn can wait until he has definite proof that Claude uses marijuana and then separate him. Such proof could come from the police if they arrested him for it. He could have the company nurse observe Claude for suspicious behavior, or he could send Claude to the company doctor on a Monday morning for a physical examination.

Vaughn can then recommend to his boss that Claude be separated because he uses drugs despite Vaughn's insistence that loyalty to the company, as well as Claude's own health, required him to avoid such a practice.

THE ESSENCE OF THIS APPROACH

Vaughn is entirely fair to Claude and doesn't take any action until Claude definitely proves this kind of disloyalty to the company.

B. Vaughn can call Claude in once more and tell him that:

- He is still getting reports on Claude's probable drug use from people without malice and with company loyalties.
- He is not interested in taking action on the basis of unsubstantiated reports of Claude's drug use.
- He *had* asked Claude to be careful, as a matter of loyalty, not to jeopardize the company by his actions.
- The persistent reports of such drug use are a symptom of carelessness (in creating an impression of use) at the very least.
- Such carelessness is disloyal to Vaughn and the company.
- The next time Vaughn gets the impression that Claude may be using drugs he will have to discharge Claude.

THE ESSENCE OF THIS APPROACH

Vaughn places the emphasis on loyalty — in avoiding at least the impression of drug use — rather than of proof of such use. Vaughn relies on the persistent reports of loyal employees and gives Claude a chance to prevent the recurrence of reports which come in only about him.

ADAPTING THESE SOLUTIONS TO YOUR OWN WORK

An assistant who uses drugs in his personal life can adversely affect the company. Even if he cannot be proven to be using them, if there is substantial evidence that he might be, it might be harmful to the company to wait for proof — as, for example, if he were arrested for it and reported in the newspapers as an employee of the company.

If you have reason to believe that one of your assistants might be using drugs outside the company, call him in and tell him:

- I'm not accusing you of anything.
- The reports I hear are too probable in their truth for me to disregard them.
- I ask you, as a matter of loyalty to me, not to let anything that you do in your personal life embarrass or hurt the company, to say nothing of yourself.
- If you cannot show me this loyalty I will have to treat it in the same way as I would any disloyalty from any of my men.

SITUATION NUMBER 83 — **The disloyal assistant who falsifies the reason for being absent from work.**

INCIDENT

Felix Edlin is a foreman in Hiram Wrigley's department.

One day Felix phones in shortly before his shift is to start and tells Hiram that he woke up ill and was going to spend the day at home. Hiram expresses his sympathy, asks whether there is anything Felix needs and, when he is told that there isn't, asks Felix to take care of himself. Hiram then makes the necessary arrangements to cover Felix's work.

A few days later, when Hiram is having lunch with the sales manager, the latter casually mentions that he'd been at a nearby race track with a customer and had seen Felix there, although Felix hadn't seen him.

Hiram thanks the sales manager but makes no further comment on the matter. He then checks with the personnel manager and finds that Felix has been absent, with apparently valid excuses, on several other occasions.

ALTERNATE SOLUTIONS

A. Hiram can call Felix in and tell him what the sales manager told him, although he doesn't have to indicate who his informant was. If Felix denies the statement, Hiram can say that he's glad that Felix is as loyal as Hiram has always felt him to be. Hiram can then watch Felix's absences very carefully and include a visit by the nurse the next time that Felix reports in ill, the rationale being that the company is interested in his health and wants to help where it can.

THE ESSENCE OF THIS APPROACH

Hiram gives Felix every opportunity to prove his loyalty at the same time that Hiram exercises greater care in future, similar situations.

B. Hiram can call Felix in and say:

- You have a record of absences which didn't cause me to doubt your loyalty because they were not too frequent and there were always valid-sounding explanations.
- Your last absence is open to some kind of question about which I'd just as soon not go into details yet.
- What I'm concerned with is my ability to continue to trust you.
- Tell me exactly what was the matter with you the last time you were absent.

If Felix owns up to the deception, Hiram can lecture him

very severely and tell him that the next time that Felix displays disloyalty of this kind he'll have to go. If Felix persists in the story of illness Hiram will have to accept it and say no more to him about it, except that he will be much more careful in the future to investigate repeated absences.

THE ESSENCE OF THIS APPROACH

Hiram hints at Felix's possible disloyalty and gives him a chance to own up. Hiram's action then depends on Felix's response.

C. Hiram can ask the sales manager whether he'd be willing to help him if he needed him to talk with him in Felix's presence. If the sales manager is willing, Hiram asks Felix — alone — whether he'd really been ill that day. If Felix says that he had been, Hiram rejoins that he has reason to believe that that is not so, but wants to be fair.

If Felix still persists in his story, Hiram calls the sales manager in and confronts Felix with the story. Hiram thanks the sales manager and talks to Felix again, alone. If Felix still insists that he wasn't at the track, Hiram decides whom to believe and acts accordingly. If Felix owns up to the deception, Hiram decides whether to give him another chance.

THE ESSENCE OF THIS APPROACH

Hiram comes as close as he can to arriving at the truth of the situation and makes the best possible judgment and decision that he can under the circumstances.

ADAPTING THESE SOLUTIONS TO YOUR OWN WORK

Truthfulness in an assistant is one of the most significant aspects of the loyalty you have a right to expect from him. In the first instance you take such honesty for granted and work on that assumption.

If, however, the reliability of any one assistant is brought into question by someone who is himself quite reliable, you must investigate. Try to be as fair as possible in this, but if you can't come to a clear conclusion about the current provocation, be careful in the future until you can satisfy yourself about the true state of that assistant's loyalty.

SITUATION NUMBER 84 — The disloyal assistant who resigns his job and then wants to return.

INCIDENT

Jay Farley has been working for the company for over ten years as a managing engineer. During a period of high wages and salaries in the local labor market, he accepted a position with another company at a considerable increase in pay. He gave two weeks' notice.

A year later, the company to which he had transferred began to lay off newer employees and Jay was jobless. He appealed to his former boss, Todd Wallach, to take him back in any position which was available at a compensation and set of duties comparable to what he had had before leaving the company.

ALTERNATE SOLUTIONS

A. If Jay's services are really vital to the company and the vacancy has been difficult to fill, Todd can talk to Jay as follows:

- We could use you, although in a different job.
- I'd like you to know, however, that you'll be working under the cloud of suspicion that you'll leave us again.
- We'll therefore be careful not to put ourselves in a position where your departure once more could hurt us.
- If you want the job under those conditions it's yours.

THE ESSENCE OF THIS APPROACH

Todd emphasizes the effects on Jay of his disloyalty and puts him on notice that he has to demonstrate a greater loyalty than he did previously.

B. Todd can have a long talk with Jay and try to come to some kind of firm conviction that Jay can now be loyal. If Todd comes to that conclusion he can rehire Jay and give him another chance to advance in proportion to demonstrated loyalty.

THE ESSENCE OF THIS APPROACH

Todd gives both Jay and the company another chance to benefit from the relationship under more secure loyalty conditions.

C. Todd can tell Jay that he regrets that he can't take him back in any job because to do so violates both good management and company policy. He explains that experience has shown that once an assistant demonstrates disloyalty to his company by leaving it he can't really be trusted to regain and maintain the kind of loyalty required from its employees.

THE ESSENCE OF THIS APPROACH

Todd avoids taking a chance on investing company time and assets once more in an assistant who has already demonstrated disloyalty.

ADAPTING THESE SOLUTIONS TO YOUR OWN WORK

As a general rule, it is not good policy to rehire an employee who has left in order to go to work for another company. Such action on his part demonstrates a selfishness which is inconsistent with the company man from whom loyalty is demanded.

The only time when this policy can be bypassed with impunity is when the man's services are needed badly and the company takes him back without committing or exposing itself.

SITUATION NUMBER 85 — The disloyal assistant who feels that a new duty is beneath his dignity.

INCIDENT

LeRoy Geer had been company dispatcher, responsible for the planning of the best utilization of the company's vehicles. His work had dealt largely with the relevant paperwork, phone calls and occasional visits to the loading-unloading areas.

His boss, traffic manager Marcelle Hammer, reorganized

the department and decided that the people-management of the company truck drivers should be added to LeRoy's duties since LeRoy had clearly demonstrated that he had sufficient time to assume this new responsibility.

Marcelle told this to LeRoy, who didn't deny that he had the time to take on the additional tasks but objected that he didn't like to deal with the drivers. He said that they were a rough lot and that having to work with them would be below his dignity as a management employee of the company on his level.

ALTERNATE SOLUTIONS

A. Marcelle can try to convince LeRoy that he is mistaken about the lack of dignity involved.

THE ESSENCE OF THIS APPROACH

Marcelle tries to undo the disloyal aspects of Leroy's feelings about the new duties.

B. Marcelle can speak to LeRoy as follows:

- The drivers have to be under a capable supervisor.
- The reorganization that I had to go through recently made it necessary for me to assign them to someone else who was capable.
- You're the best man for the job.
- You should view it as another facet of your loyalty to me and take it on willingly and even enthusiastically.

THE ESSENCE OF THIS APPROACH

Marcelle appeals directly to Leroy's loyalty to overcome the reservations he has about assuming the new duties.

ADAPTING THESE SOLUTIONS TO YOUR OWN WORK

When you have to add new duties to an assistant, you will, of course, try to fit them to the right man. Before doing so, however, it might be well to do a selling job on him. This is not to say that you won't go through with the assignment if he isn't sold.

If an assistant feels that the new duties which you want to give him are beneath his dignity, try to convince him that this isn't so, but if he still feels that way, appeal to his loyalty to adapt himself to them. If even that doesn't work and you still need to have him perform them, make it plain to him that his attitude must in no way adversely affect his success.

16

How to Handle
The Old-Time Employee

In the following situations notice that an old-time employee, while he may be a continuing asset to the company, often becomes a problem. He's more apt to resist change. He may be unable to keep up with new methods. He may be looking forward to retirement, unhindered by upsetting applecarts. Notice how the manager must try to get the best and most out of that kind of employee while being as humane as possible.

SITUATION NUMBER 86 — The old-time employee who has become dead wood.

INCIDENT

Mitch Ireland had started with the company thirty years ago. He'd advanced steadily until he became a supervisor of telephone order takers.

A few years ago the company converted its telephone order entry setup to a computer. Mitch had resisted this but lost the battle. Mitch's boss, Otto Jaffe, tried in every way possible to win Mitch over to the new way, but Mitch was unmovable. His management activities deteriorated to the point where the only thing he would do was fill out reports, based on information he got from his men. He spent all of the rest of his time not devoted to those reports to walking about and talking to his cronies, or to sitting at his desk and killing time.

ALTERNATE SOLUTIONS

A. Otto can insist that Mitch retire early at the maximum pension that the company's plan allows.

THE ESSENCE OF THIS APPROACH

Otto gives Mitch the next best opportunity to doing his job right (which he will not do), being as humanitarian as possible to Mitch and making it possible to replace him with an effective supervisor.

B. Otto can try to find a job unrelated to his present job for Mitch which will yield *some* valuable productivity, and move him into the new post under circumstances which might be considered, if not a promotion, at least not demeaning.

THE ESSENCE OF THIS APPROACH

Otto tries to get maximum use out of Mitch's experience in a post where his attitude toward his present job won't be a hindrance.

C. Otto can tell his own boss that:

- Mitch is unchangeable in his present job by present motivations.
- He wants to make one last try at getting Mitch to become useful.
- He wants authorization to tell Mitch that he's being given one last chance to measure up to his job, subject to separation if he doesn't make the grade.

Otto can then tell this to Mitch and watch his work carefully. If Mitch doesn't initiate and maintain the desired kind of improvement, Otto will separate Mitch.

THE ESSENCE OF THIS APPROACH

Otto gives Mitch one last chance to change and become useful, under last-chance sanction. If Mitch doesn't make the grade, Otto is rid of dead wood.

ADAPTING THESE SOLUTIONS TO YOUR OWN WORK

The best way to deal with dead wood, of course, is to prevent an employee from becoming such. The best approach to that is to evaluate your assistants continually and come to appropriate decisions as soon as it is likely that one of them is soon to become and remain dead wood.

If, however, you inherit dead wood from a predecessor who didn't follow that course, try to get the man to change through normal motivation. If you can't, the most important thing is to get him away at once from the position he's hindering; then do whatever is most humane, consistent with company profit.

SITUATION NUMBER 87 — The old-time employee who resents the new hire.

INCIDENT

Salvatore Valentino has been a production foreman for a long time; his boss is Tad Jagels.

With the approval of the manufacturing manager and the president, Tad has hired an industrial engineer, Seth Kantor, to make a study of production standards and come up with suggestions on an ongoing basis for improving productivity in all the departments, including Sal's.

When Seth begins to visit Sal's area and ask authorized questions, Sal — according to reliable reports — engages in the following practices at one time or another:

- Suggestions to his men that they not cooperate with Seth.
- Reluctance to answer Seth's questions to him.
- Misleading answers.
- Snide remarks to other foreman about the young whippersnapper who thinks he knows more than the old-timers and will probably cause a great deal of trouble.

ALTERNATE SOLUTIONS

A. Tad can sit down with Sal and talk to him like this:

- I understand that you feel that Seth is not a healthy influence around here.
- Please give me your specific statements of the harm you think he's doing and the waste of company money you think he represents.

Since Sal will not be able to meet this challenge, Tad can then say to Sal:

- Since you have no real basis for your criticism, I'm going to ask you to stop talking against Seth and urging your men not to cooperate.
- Your job as foreman requires that attitude and action from you.

THE ESSENCE OF THIS APPROACH

Tad puts Sal on the spot and makes him admit that he is really opposed to something new and not the real benefits to the company. Tad reinforces this by a direct order to Sal to stop his undesirable practices.

B. Tad can sit down with Sal and try to explain to him why Seth's work is so important to all concerned, including Sal. Tad tries to win Sal over to the new position and its incumbent.

THE ESSENCE OF THIS APPROACH

Tad tries to make Sal see the true picture and tries to motivate him to the proper stance.

C. Tad can call Sal in and speak to him this way:

- I was responsible for bringing Seth in because I was — and am — convinced that his work would be and is essential.
- You are fighting Seth as hard as you can, for whatever reasons of your own.
- In doing so you are fighting me and the company as well, and doing yourself discredit in my eyes and those of all the people to whom you talk against Seth.

- I cannot permit any of my foremen to do this.
- Either learn to agree with and support Seth's mission or give him 100 percent cooperation even if you don't feel like it.
- Your continued failure to do this would be inconsistent with your value to the company and me as a foreman.

THE ESSENCE OF THIS APPROACH

Tad makes Sal see that opposition to Seth is opposition to Tad, and that it must stop if Sal is to continue to be a foreman in the company.

ADAPTING THESE SOLUTIONS TO YOUR OWN WORK

If an old-time employee under you resents a new employee hired by you for an important position, you had best try first to find out why the resentment arose and how to remove it.

If you can't get the assistant to stop resenting the new hire, at least insist that his continued repetition of criticism cease and that he do everything that must be done to cooperate with him.

The crucial point is that the new hire is doing what *you* want him to do, and every one of your assistants *must* do what *you* wish if they are to continue to function as your assistants.

SITUATION NUMBER 88 — The old-time employee who is jealous of the younger employee.

INCIDENT

Carmine Guerra has been in the accounting department for twenty years or so. He had started as a bookkeeper and had advanced to be the supervisor of one of the accounting departments. He had never gone beyond high school but was a very competent man for his job.

Chris Lancaster came to the company right out of his college with a degree in accounting, and was almost immediately put in charge of another section of the accounting department.

Both men worked under Stu Madoff.

Before Chris came to the company Carmine had felt that he

was Stu's most valuable and important man. Now he hears Stu talking with Chris in conference or at meetings in a professional way that Carmine has never enjoyed and can't because of his lack of academic accounting knowledge.

Carmine begins to lay traps for Chris in order to show him up and often backbites among his people against Chris.

ALTERNATE SOLUTIONS

A. Stu can call Carmine in and talk to him along these lines:

- I've noticed lately that you seem to be waging a war of prestige and importance against Chris.
- I think I know why you're doing it but I want to assure you that there is no need for such action.
- Each of you is important to me in his own way.
- You're too valuable and loyal an assistant to me to continue to behave this way and I wish you'd stop it.

THE ESSENCE OF THIS APPROACH

Stu presents the situation to Carmine squarely, appeals to his security and loyalty and urges him to stop manifesting and feeling jealousy.

B. Stu can call each of them in, at first separately. To Chris he can say: Carmine is jealous of you, but he's a valued employee. Try to build him up and get him to work with you wherever possible, as though you need his help and advice, because he's been around so much longer than you.

To Carmine he can then say: Chris is new here and doesn't know all the ropes. I'd appreciate it if you gave him a hand and helped him learn some of what only you — between the two of you — know.

THE ESSENCE OF THIS APPROACH

Stu gets Chris to make Carmine feel important and then does the same himself.

C. Stu can call the two of them in together from time to time to ask their joint help in undertaking certain activities. He can appeal to each of them for help in what is obviously his forte, and emphasize the need for cooperation because each complements the other.

THE ESSENCE OF THIS APPROACH

Stu plays each one up in the other's presence, thus emphasizing their joint importance to him.

ADAPTING THESE SOLUTIONS TO YOUR OWN WORK

If you have an old-time employee who is valuable to you but he is jealous of a younger employee, you must try to build the old-time employee's self-esteem. This is best accomplished by getting the younger man to cooperate in this attempt and then bringing them together in order to convince the older one that he has no real reason for his jealousy.

SITUATION NUMBER 89 — The old-time employee who is close to your boss.

INCIDENT

Sol Magee had been a superintendent in one of the production departments for about two years. Conrad Olson has been head of another production department for over twenty-five years.

Conrad is very close to their mutual boss, Evan Cammack. They always eat lunch together — alone — and frequently socialize at home.

Sol often has difficulty getting in to see Ev on fairly important matters, while Conrad has no such difficulty. Sol has to wait what he considers too long for requisitions to be signed by Ev, where Conrad gets his signed at once. Conrad gets the best men when a vacancy occurs in his department; Sol gets what's left.

ALTERNATE SOLUTIONS

A. Sol can go straight to Ev and tell him exactly what he thinks is the situation, pointing out that he finds the setup intolerable and asking Ev to put a stop to it.

THE ESSENCE OF THIS APPROACH

Sol shows Ev that he has the courage to stand up for what he believes right and won't put up with the setup.

B. Sol can sit down with Ev and:

- Tell him the impression he is getting about Conrad's being given preferred treatment at his — Sol's — expense.
- Say that he is probably wrong about that inference and wants Ev to assure him that he *is* wrong.

THE ESSENCE OF THIS APPROACH

Sol gives Ev a chance to correct the inequity without accusing Ev of wrongdoing.

C. Sol can tell Ev that he wants a transfer to another department.

When Ev asks him why, Sol can say:

- I get the feeling that I'm not acceptable to you, for the following reasons: . . .
- I know that I have a contribution to make to the company.
- I can't make that contribution as long as I have that feeling.
- I think it would be best for both of us and the company if I worked somewhere else.

THE ESSENCE OF THIS APPROACH

Sol places the blame on himself, gives Ev a chance to reform and makes it plain to Ev that the chips are down.

ADAPTING THESE SOLUTIONS TO YOUR OWN WORK

If you have reason to believe that one of your fellows is being given preferential treatment by your mutual boss, make sure that you are competent and prepared to do your best, document the reasons for that feeling and go to your boss.

Tell him as tactfully as you can, what you think and that you can't work effectively under those conditions. Leave the solution up to him, but make it clear that you are firm in your resolve about it.

SITUATION NUMBER 90 — The old-time employee who has lost ambition for promotion.

INCIDENT

Gavin Darden has been with the company for twenty years. He started out as a clerk and finally was made supervisor over a number of clerks. He's had this position for five years.

Gavin's boss, Julian Edwards, has wanted to promote Gavin on a number of occasions when openings occured that he thought Gavin could fill with a greater contribution than in his present job.

Gavin has continually turned down Julian's offers, saying that he was too old (forty-five) and too set in his ways to change, being completely satisfied to continue in his present job until retirement.

ALTERNATE SOLUTIONS

A. If Gavin is doing the best job as supervisor in his section that anyone could do, Julian can continue him in the present post and refrain from offering him any additional opportunities for promotion. The only thing that Julian has to be careful about is that Gavin's static position where he is doesn't prevent any of his deserving clerk assistants from being promoted when the occasion arises. In such a situation, they can be upgraded in different sections.

THE ESSENCE OF THIS APPROACH

Julian keeps a satisfactory supervisor where he can make a valuable contribution and still doesn't discourage others from aspiring to rise.

B. If Gavin's attitude toward not rising begins to reflect itself in a diminution of his effectiveness as a supervisor, Julian must find a way to remove him from that post without demeaning him too noticeably and use his experience and services wherever they make the best contribution to the company.

THE ESSENCE OF THIS APPROACH

A failure to advance might be synonymous with a failure to do well in the current job. If this turns out to be the case, Julian must remove Gavin from his post as supervisor and use him where he makes that contribution which is consistent with profitability and Gavin's upward limits.

C. If Gavin's unwillingness to rise means that his assistants will have no opportunity to advance because one of the major vacancies would occur in their own section, Julian must decide:

- Whether any one of those assistants is so being prevented from rising.
- If so, whether it's more important to the company to give him a chance to rise than it is to keep Gavin where he is.

THE ESSENCE OF THIS APPROACH

Julian looks out not only for Gavin's interest but also for that of others who might contribute less to the company if they can't rise because Gavin won't.

ADAPTING THESE SOLUTIONS TO YOUR OWN WORK

Not every employee is ambitious to rise nor should he be. You want some assistants for specific jobs where they are perfectly content and make valuable contributions. You want others who want to rise and deserve to do so. What you need is the proper numerical balance between the two kinds of employees so that you always have the proper supply of each kind.

If, however, you believe that a particular employee *should* advance and he doesn't want to, keep him where he is only if that won't prevent others who deserve to from advancing. If you can't help them to rise because of the unambitious one's being where he is, move him to a place where he can make the kind of contribution both you and he can live with and give the others a chance to advance.

17

How to Handle The Employee With Personal Problems

In the following situations notice that the manager must interest himself in his assistants' personal problems either when they bring them up or when it's obvious to the manager that something is bothering them which is affecting their contributions at work. You must, however, be careful not to go beyond certain bounds in what you do about their personal problems, as illustrated by those situations.

SITUATION NUMBER 91 — The employee with personal problems who is frequently absent or late because of home troubles.

INCIDENT

Abel Zinn is a capable and conscientious foreman, but he is often late to work (with advance notice) and absent from work (also with advance notice). His boss, Wilbur Farrell, finally questions Abel about this excessive record of undesirable punctuality and unattendance at work.

Abel tells Wilbur that his oldest son, age sixteen, is behaving in a peculiar manner: he comes home late in the night, contrary to instructions from home, often dazed (possibly by marijuana) and occasionally drunk. His son also frequently wakes up early in the morning sick or disturbed, requiring not only Abel's wife's attention but also his own.

ALTERNATE SOLUTIONS

A. Wilbur can ask Abel whether he would like any help from Wilbur. If Abel agrees, Wilbur can ask the company's personnel manager to meet with him and see how he — the personnel manager — can help, within the limits of proper company assistance in such cases.

If Abel turns down Wilbur's offer, the latter must point out to him that in such a case Abel has to solve the problem himself, and that much as this grieves Wilbur, Abel simply must come to work on time and without excessive absence.

THE ESSENCE OF THIS APPROACH

Wilbur offers to help Abel within proper limits. If Abel turns this offer down, Wilbur has no choice but to insist that Abel must solve the problem on his own but *must* follow a regular pattern of punctuality and regularity of attendance at work.

B. Wilbur can ask Abel whether there isn't any way that Abel can leave the problem to his wife during the working day and take care of it himself after or before hours. The accompanying requirement must be that Abel's home problems mustn't interfere with his effectiveness on the job.

THE ESSENCE OF THIS APPROACH

Wilbur stays out of the problem altogether, although he suggests that Abel try to allocate his time and attention properly between home and work.

C. Wilbur can suggest to Abel that he take a leave of absence from work until he has the problem in hand.

THE ESSENCE OF THIS APPROACH

Abel would then be in a position to try to solve the problem once and for all and come back to work when it was solved.

ADAPTING THESE SOLUTIONS TO YOUR OWN WORK

Every employee must come to work punctually and regularly except when, on occasion, he simply cannot. If, however, the frequency of lateness and absence goes beyond bearable proportions, his boss must do something about it.

The first step, of course, is to find out why the irregularity is occurring. If the reason is personal home problems, you should offer the help of the personnel manager, who will know how far the company can go in helping the troubled employee. If this doesn't work for whatever reason, a leave of absence may help solve the problem.

In any case, you must always feel and show interest in your assistant's problem, but nothing must interfere with his regularity and punctuality of attendance.

SITUATION NUMBER 92 — The employee with personal problems who is not in good physical condition.

INCIDENT

Angelo Paoli is a clerical supervisor working under Walter Garber. Angelo had always been very energetic and conscientious as well as loyal and competent.

Angelo's job required him to move about a great deal all of the time. One day he suffered a heart attack and had to be away from work for several weeks. His doctor said that he could then go back to work but that he had to take it easy for the rest of his working life.

Angelo explained all of this to Walter before he came back to work.

ALTERNATE SOLUTIONS

A. Walter can put Angelo back into the same job he had before, rearrange the work physically so as not to tax his strength unduly and caution Angelo to do the best he can without risking another attack.

THE ESSENCE OF THIS APPROACH

Walter makes it possible for a faithful employee to continue to do the best he can, with minimal interference with the company's productivity needs.

B. Walter can put Angelo into a different job not calling for such exertions as would tend to hurt him, but one which would be filled by Angelo with maximum/optimum company profitability.

THE ESSENCE OF THIS APPROACH

Angelo can continue to be useful to the company and there is no need to change essential duties in the company.

C. Walter can recommend that Angelo be given early disability retirement.

THE ESSENCE OF THIS APPROACH

The company relieves itself of any possible responsibility for Angelo's becoming ill again and avoids damage to company productivity.

ADAPTING THESE SOLUTIONS TO YOUR OWN WORK

When an employee becomes ill it's important to discover the extent to which his recovery permits him to resume working at your company. If a reliable doctor says that there has been no adverse effect on his ability to continue to work exactly as before, then there is no reason why he can't be put back to maximum/optimum productivity.

On the other hand, if there is a reasonable chance that his illness has caused him to have to work less assiduously for the rest of his career, you have to balance several items and decide what's best for both the company and the employee:

- For the company: what's the dollar cost/yield from his limited continuance in the company?
- For the employee: what's best for him from both a health standpoint (mental as well as physical) and a financial one?

SITUATION NUMBER 93 — The employee with personal problems who needs more money than his merited salary.

INCIDENT

Werner Hammond is a department head. His boss is Aubrey Irvin. Werner has been with the company a long time and has always done exceptional work. Lately, however, Werner has been moving about the company with a preoccupied look and has been neglecting to meet certain commitments on time. Since this is most unusual for Werner, Aubrey asks him what the trouble is. Werner explains that his oldest son has been traveling around with an undesirable crowd, despite Werner's every effort to put a stop to it, and that the boy had gotten into trouble which has led to a dilemma for Werner.

When Aubrey presses Werner to go into greater detail, he says that the boy's latest escapade led to a great deal of damage to a man's property, and that the judge had given Werner two alternatives: either pay the man back for all of his losses or send the boy to a correctional institution for an indefinite term as a juvenile delinquent.

Werner assures Aubrey that the boy has had no previous arrests, but adds that he — Werner — hasn't the money needed to pay the injured man what the judge has assessed, either in one payment or (as the man has indicated his willingness) in five payments.

ALTERNATE SOLUTIONS

A. Aubrey can ask the company to assume the obligation for Werner and arrange to take stated sums out of his salary in the coming year(s) to make up for the loan.

THE ESSENCE OF THIS APPROACH

The company makes it possible for Werner to resume his profitable contribution to it without the concern which has been interfering with this.

B. Aubrey can refer Werner to the company's personnel manager for advice and help on how to solve his financial problem and urge him to do so because of the need for a clear mind on the job.

THE ESSENCE OF THIS APPROACH

Aubrey offers to have the company help Werner with no possible financial loss to it.

C. Aubrey can tell Werner that:

- He genuinely regrets the dilemma which Werner faces.
- He regrets that the company's policy prevents any financial help to Werner in that kind of situation.
- He regrets that the company cannot assume even to advise him in the matter.
- Werner will have to make a special effort to avoid having his personal problem interfere with his work.

THE ESSENCE OF THIS APPROACH

Aubrey makes it plain to Werner that this kind of personal problem cannot be assumed even in part by the company, and that Werner must not permit that problem to hurt his contribution to the company.

ADAPTING THESE SOLUTIONS TO YOUR OWN WORK

When an assistant has a personal financial problem the company has two major alternatives:

- If company policy permits, it may either help him financially or advise him where to get that help.
- If company policy does not permit this, it must express sympathy but insist that the assistant's work must not be adversely affected by his personal problem.

SITUATION NUMBER 94 — The employee with personal problems whose wife makes him dissatisfied with his job.

INCIDENT

Boris Kaplon has been with the company for three years. He had been hired by Sebastian James into a high managerial capacity, away from a company where Boris — though dissatisfied with the company's policies — had been a vice president. Boris had not been made a vice president in his new job.

One day Boris comes to Sebastian and says:

- I'm very happy with my job here, but I'm having a problem with my wife.
- In the last community where we worked I was, as you know, a vice president of the company.
- This gave my wife a certain prestige in that community, although it made no difference to me.
- My wife feels demeaned in our new community because I no longer have that title, and she has been very unhappy about it.
- I don't want any more money, but couldn't you give me that title for her sake and my peace of mind?

ALTERNATE SOLUTIONS

A. Sebastian can tell Boris that he'll do the best he can to get the title awarded to him. He can then do so and so inform Boris.

THE ESSENCE OF THIS APPROACH

Sebastian removes the problem facing his faithful and valuable employee, thus assuring that that problem won't diminish the latter's effectiveness.

B. Sebastian can tell Boris:

- I sympathize with your situation and would like to help you solve it.
- I cannot do as you request, however, because it's against company policy.
- I must insist that you see to it that your wife's dissatisfaction with your situation doesn't in any way interfere with your continued maximum/optimum contribution to our profit through your fulfillment of your responsibilities.

THE ESSENCE OF THIS APPROACH

Sebastian makes it plain that the company cannot permit that kind of problem to interfere with Boris's continued value to it.

ADAPTING THESE SOLUTIONS TO YOUR OWN WORK

An assistant's wife's feelings about her husband's job can have an effect on his contribution to the company. You should, of course, make it your business to know what those feelings are. If she is legitimately dissatisfied, you should do all you can to make her happy again, but if what it takes to make her satisfied is inconsistent with company policy — or would be an unwarranted favoritism to her husband — you'll simply have to tell him that you can't help him.

In all cases he must be made aware of the fact that he must not permit her dissatisfaction to prevent him from doing his job correctly.

In addition, before you hire an important assistant you would do well to interview his wife and see what her attitudes are toward his proposed status. Also, if she begins to express dissatisfaction after he's been hired, you might probe to see whether this is going to lead to his looking around for another job before you can take the initiative to separate him.

SITUATION NUMBER 95 — The employee with personal problems who can't stay at work later than the regular time.

INCIDENT

Brian Lande is a foreman on the first shift from 8 A.M. to 4 P.M. The company policy is that foremen are paid a salary of such a nature that even if the wage employees work and are paid for overtime, the foremen — who must work along with them without overtime pay — always wind up at the end of the year with a sizable excess in remuneration over their men.

Lately Brian's superintendent, Sig Magill, has authorized

overtime work for most of the foremen's departments. Brian's people have had to put in from two to three hours additional on each of several days.

On one occasion, when Sig has requested that Brian plan overtime work for the next day, Brian tells Sig that he can't stay, either then or too frequently in any one month. Brian's reported reason is that his wife isn't too well and that he has to help her prepare for the children's dinner and other family requirements.

ALTERNATE SOLUTIONS

A. Sig can arrange for another foreman to take Brian's overtime shift work, paying that other foreman — out of Brian's salary — a reasonable amount of money for his extra time.

THE ESSENCE OF THIS APPROACH

Sig retains a valuable foreman and gives another foreman an opportunity to earn more money at no additional cost to the company.

B. Sig can arrange for Brian to be moved to another job which doesn't require overtime hours, even if this represents less prestige and perhaps less salary.

THE ESSENCE OF THIS APPROACH

Sig makes it possible for Brian to continue to work for the company without having the problem revealed by him to be his as foreman.

C. Sig can tell Brian that he will have to make other arrangements to solve his personal problem and that he simply must work overtime whenever the company's needs call for this.

THE ESSENCE OF THIS APPROACH

Sig insists that Brian must do what the job calls for and not let his personal situation prevent it from being done properly.

ADAPTING THESE SOLUTIONS TO YOUR OWN WORK

Before you hire a foreman, make it plain to him that his job calls for him to work along with his men whenever necessary, even after hours.

If, after he has been hired, he says that a situation has arisen making it impossible for him to do this, you have to weigh various factors and decide which one or combination is best for you:

- The fact that a foreman has to work alongside of his men whenever they are working.
- The fact that aside from vacations and unavoidable short illnesses, the men work best when it is their own foreman who supervises them.
- The desire not to cause unhappiness to a valuable employee, especially if this might interfere with his effectiveness.

18

How to Handle The Assistant Who Is Always Too Busy

In the following situations note that the first step is to find out whether the business is legitimate and/or necessary. If is it neither, the solution lies in pointing this out to the assistant and helping him to make or have the necessary time. If, however, he really is too busy, his work load must be re-evaluated and he must not be asked to assume more tasks than any reasonably competent employee in his position should be expected to be able to complete satisfactorily.

SITUATION NUMBER 96 — The assistant who is always too busy to come to meetings on time.

INCIDENT

Carter Naylor is a department head, working for Rufus Olcott.

Almost always, when Rufus calls a meeting — sufficiently well in advance — to which Carter has been invited, he fails to show up on time. His excuse is always that he is so busy, or has suddenly become involved in something that has just come up, that he can't get away in time to be prompt to the meeting.

ALTERNATE SOLUTIONS

A. Rufus can point out to Carter that he is the only one of the assistants who is consistently late to meetings, and that he must simply so organize his time and work that he comes as promptly as the others.

THE ESSENCE OF THIS APPROACH

Rufus refuses to accept Carter's excuse, saying that Carter must conform like the others.

B. Rufus can make a study of Carter's work load and work habits to see whether his excuse is justified. If it is, he can re-arrange Carter's load accordingly.

If, however, it is Carter's work habits which cause the lateness, Rufus must take the steps necessary to train Carter in more acceptable habits.

THE ESSENCE OF THIS APPROACH

Rufus tries to ascertain the real situation and act accordingly.

C. Rufus can ask Carter to send a trusted assistant to meetings when Carter realizes that he's going to be late. This assistant can brief Carter on what he missed when he finally does arrive.

THE ESSENCE OF THIS APPROACH

Carter can continue to take care of important matters without either holding up the meetings or missing important details.

ADAPTING THESE SOLUTIONS TO YOUR OWN WORK

You should call only that number of meetings which is essential for your effectiveness and invite to those meetings only those people whose participation is important to the company. You must also set meeting times for the smallest interference with your assistants' schedules. Finally, you ought to give them as much advance notice as possible.

Once you've done all of this, each of your assistants must be made to understand that he must be prompt for the good of all concerned. If any one assistant is consistently late to meetings, he is either too overloaded or too poorly organized, either of which situation must be resolved.

SITUATION NUMBER 97 — The assistant who is always too busy to follow proper priorities of work due.

INCIDENT

Clark Panken is one of Reggie Wyatt's supervisors. Clark is very conscientious and competent, but he's always very busy.

Once he gets started on a project he likes to follow through on it until he has finished it. He often fails, however, to meet deadlines established for and communicated to him by Reggie.

ALTERNATE SOLUTIONS

A. Reggie can insist that Clark draw up and present to him a schedule of all of his projects, indicating when he intends to complete each of them. If the schedule then looks like one which is inconsistent with Clark's ability to meet Reggie's deadlines for him, he can help Clark rearrange the schedules in advance in order to assure the proper meeting of deadlines.

THE ESSENCE OF THIS APPROACH

Reggie takes preventive measures to make it probable that Clark will arrange his work according to Reggie's deadlines.

B. Reggie can refrain from giving Clark more than one project at a time and can insist that Clark not assume any projects other than those approved by Reggie. Reggie can then see to it that the proper priorities are observed.

THE ESSENCE OF THIS APPROACH

Reggie replaces Clark's decisions on priorities with his own, thus avoiding the possibility that Clark would get bogged down.

ADAPTING THESE SOLUTIONS TO YOUR OWN WORK

You must make perfectly clear to your assistants any priorities that you want them to follow; then insist that these priorities be met.

It's a good idea, in general, to check up from time to time on whether their work is progressing in such a way that they will meet the deadlines you've established. For those assistants who seem unable to do their own scheduling along lines you find essential, you must then provide some kind of safeguard against their laggings. Either insist on advance scheduling approved by you or don't let them work or even plan on more than one project at a time.

SITUATION NUMBER 98 — The assistant who is always too busy to manage his men.

INCIDENT

Dirk Ramsey is a supervisor in the accounting department. He works for the controller, Rafe Walsh. Dirk has seven assistants.

Rafe is not satisfied with the quantity or quality of the work being turned out by Dirk's section, and yet he notices that Dirk is always busy at his desk and never wastes a moment. Rafe discovers that the problem is that Dirk doesn't take the time to manage his people and that their work is either careless or of unacceptable quality as a result. When Rafe points this out to Dirk, the latter replies that he is too busy with his own work to be able to manage his assistants properly.

ALTERNATE SOLUTIONS

A. Rafe can make a study of the work that Dirk does himself. If he doesn't delegate enough, this can be pointed out to him. If his own undelegable work is really excessive, this can be cut down.

THE ESSENCE OF THIS APPROACH

Rafe sees to it that Dirk is not justifiably so overburdened that he really doesn't have time to manage his people properly.

B. Rafe can ask Dirk to keep a record of the activities that he himself engages in, noting the time taken for each activity. Dirk can then be asked to turn this record in to Rafe after a reasonable period.

THE ESSENCE OF THIS APPROACH

Rafe puts the burden of discovering the trouble on Dirk.

C. Rafe can call Dirk in and say to him:

- The work of your section is unsatisfactory.
- It doesn't matter to me why this is so, as long as it is so, unless it's my fault.
- The work of your assistants must meet your standards and you must meet my standards.
- As a general rule, assistants must be properly managed or they cannot be expected to do their work well.
- Your major job is to manage them thus.
- Either point out to me how I am responsible for their poor work or see to it that your entire section — including you — gives me the results I want — consistently.

THE ESSENCE OF THIS APPROACH

Rafe points out to Dirk what his management responsibility is, insisting that Dirk meet it.

ADAPTING THESE SOLUTIONS TO YOUR OWN WORK

Don't so overload an assistant that he has to do too many things by himself. His major job is to delegate and manage. If the results of any one assistant's department are consistently unacceptable, find out why. If the major reason is that he is so busy doing his own work that he isn't managing them properly, find out whether this is justifiable. If it is, rearrange his work load. If it isn't, remind him that his main job is management.

SITUATION NUMBER 99 — The assistant who is always too busy to make important decisions.

INCIDENT

Eldridge Randolph has noticed that a number of the clerks in his department seem to have a certain amount of time with nothing to do. After discreet questioning he learns that the reason is that they have been trying to get their supervisor, Pierce Salchow, to make certain essential decisions before they can continue with specific jobs that they understand have to be done.

Eldridge asks Pierce about this and he readily admits that he hasn't made those decisions. He insists, however, that his delay was entirely justified because:

- Each decision required considerable time to make properly, and
- He was so bogged down with important tasks for Eldridge that he just didn't have the time required for the decisions.

ALTERNATE SOLUTIONS

A. Eldridge can insist that Pierce must reschedule his work in such a way that he has enough time for such decisions. He also points out that the decision making is as important as anything else that Pierce has to do.

THE ESSENCE OF THIS APPROACH

Eldridge makes it Pierce's responsibility to solve the problem.

B. Eldridge can tell Pierce that his main job is to see to it that all of his people are constantly productive in the most profitable way, and that it costs the company much more money to have them nonproductive than any failure of Pierce to finish any of his work.

THE ESSENCE OF THIS APPROACH

Eldridge restates Pierce's job duties to him and puts the burden to meet them squarely on him.

ADAPTING THESE SOLUTIONS TO YOUR OWN WORK

A supervisor must be constantly aware of the need for his assistants to be continually engaged in highly profitable productivity. He must also be aware of the fact that failure to supervise them properly can militate seriously against such productivity.

While a supervisor's assistants must exercise a certain amount of judgment and initiative, there may be certain limits to the decisions that they can make, or at least that they think they can make.

In either case, if an assistant isn't working because he thinks he needs prior approval from his boss, the latter must know this before the assistant wastes any time, and the supervisor must be able to make the decision without any interference with his discharge of his other duties.

SITUATION NUMBER 100 — The assistant who is always too busy to see his own assistants.

INCIDENT

Fabian Taylor is a supervisor answering to Newell Tauber. One day, one of Fabian's assistants, Fritz Salmon, comes to see Newell and tells him:

- I've had a problem with my work which I wanted Fabian to help me solve.

- I've tried to get in to see him several times, but he always says that he can't see me then, and will I please come back some other time.

- I don't like to go over his head, but I can't do my work properly without the help I'm seeking, and I can't get it from him.

ALTERNATE SOLUTIONS

A. Newell can tell Fritz to go back to his work, do the best he can and wait for Fabian to send for him soon.

Newell then calls Fabian in and:

- Asks him why he can't see Fritz.

- Helps Fabian solve whatever problem he's having which makes him so busy.
- Insists that Fabian give Fritz all the attention he needs at once and report back on the interview.
- Cautions him not to let that kind of situation develop again.

THE ESSENCE OF THIS APPROACH

Newell helps Fabian solve his problem, saves his face, gets help for Fritz and takes steps to prevent Fabian from committing the same management error once more.

B. Newell can ask Fritz what the problem is, thank him for the initiative he has taken and tell him he'll get his help soon.

Newell then calls Fabian in and says:

- How is that work (describing what Fritz is doing at that time) coming along?
- Has it been completed? If not, why not?
- Would you please find out right away and let me know in full detail what's happening.

If Fabian doesn't admit that he's been unable or unwilling to help Fritz, he can ask him how come Fabian didn't insist on having the work finished earlier. Newell can then criticize Fabian for that, without letting on that he knows the whole story.

THE ESSENCE OF THIS APPROACH

Newell gets Fabian to admit a criticizable management error without letting on that Fritz had come to see him. This may warn Fabian that he had better make time for his assistants.

ADAPTING THESE SOLUTIONS TO YOUR OWN WORK

You should take the time to observe whether your assistants are making enough of their own time available for the proper management, help and encouragement regarding their own assistants. If you discover that they are not, find out why, prevent this from happening again and emphasize to them that being available to their assistants is one of their most important duties.

SITUATION NUMBER 101 — The assistant who is always too busy to read important reports.

INCIDENT

Gary Murphy works as an office manager for Hubbard Lee. As Gary puts certain documents in Hubbard's "in" box and Hubbard reads them, he discovers that many of them are a bit outdated in the procedures governing them.

He finally calls Gary in and says:

- Please look at these documents which you sent me.
- They don't represent the latest procedures issued in the report we all got from the controller last week.
- How come?

Gary says he's sorry about that, but he's been so busy getting out his department's paperwork he hasn't had the time to read that report.

ALTERNATE SOLUTIONS

A. Hubbard can ask Gary what help he needs in order to make himself less busy, so that he can make the time to read important reports. Hubbard can then give Gary all appropriate help.

THE ESSENCE OF THIS APPROACH

Hubbard tries to eliminate the cause of Gary's not reading important reports.

B. Hubbard can say to Gary:

- If you are so busy that you can't handle *all* of your duties, tell me in what respects this is so and I'll try to give you the kind of help you need.
- If you were unable to read that report because you were too busy with other work, you should have told me about that before you neglected the reading.

- As a result, your work has to be done all over again.
- From now on please remember that you have to plan your work in such a way that you have time for *all* of your duties, including the reading of important reports.

THE ESSENCE OF THIS APPROACH

Newell not only offers to help Fabian to be less busy, but also chides him for failing in his very important management responsibilities.

ADAPTING THESE SOLUTIONS TO YOUR OWN WORK

If an important report is sent to one or more of your assistants, you ought to check up on whether they are reading it in a timely fashion. If you discover that some of them are *not* doing this reading appropriately, find out why and try to remedy the situation — but under no circumstances let them continue to think that that reading can wait until they do other things that they think are more important.